THE PHYSICAL SEPARATION AND RECOVERY OF METALS FROM WASTES

Process Engineering for the Chemical, Metals and Minerals Industries

Edited by Dr T. J. Veasey, School of Chemical Engineering, University of Birmingham, UK

Volume 1
THE PHYSICAL SEPARATION AND RECOVERY OF METALS FROM WASTES
by Terry J. Veasey, Robert J. Wilson and Derek M. Squires

This book is part of a series. The publisher will accept continuation orders which may be cancelled at any time and which provide for automatic billing and shipping of each title in the series upon publication. Please write for details.

THE PHYSICAL SEPARATION AND RECOVERY OF METALS FROM WASTES

Terry J. Veasey

and

Robert J. Wilson

*School of Chemical Engineering,
University of Birmingham, UK*

Derek M. Squires

*Newell Engineering Ltd,
Redditch, UK*

 CRC Press
Taylor & Francis Group
Boca Raton London New York

CRC Press is an imprint of the
Taylor & Francis Group, an **informa** business

First published 1993 by Gordon and Breach Science Publishers

Published 2019 by CRC Press
Taylor & Francis Group
6000 Broken Sound Parkway NW, Suite 300
Boca Raton, FL 33487-2742

First issued in paperback 2019

ISBN 13: 978-0-367-44974-2 (pbk)
ISBN 13: 978-2-88124-916-7 (hbk)

Visit the Taylor & Francis Web site at
http://www.taylorandfrancis.com

and the CRC Press Web site at
http://www.crcpress.com

Library of Congress Cataloging-in Publication Data

Veasey, Terry J.
    The physical separation and recovery of metals from wastes / Terry J. Veasey, Robert J. Wilson, Derek M. Squires.
        p.   ca. — (Process engineering for the chemical, metals, and minerals industries. ISSN 1066-2200; v. 1)
    Include bibliographical references (p.   ) and index.
    ISBN 2-88124-916-7
    1. Scrap metals — Recycling.   I. Wilson, Robert J.   II. Squires, Derek M.   III. Title.   IV. Series.
TS214.V43   1993
669'.042—dc20
                                                                                        93-14693
                                                                                        CIP

Contents

CHAPTER ONE

AN INTRODUCTION TO SECONDARY METALS PROCESSING

The topic of metals reclamation and recycling can be difficult to research from the published literature due to the many disparate sources of relevant data. There are a number of different interest groups concerned with the subject, including process engineers from metallurgical, chemical and minerals engineering disciplines, waste management practitioners and environmental engineers and scientists, and each of these might be concerned with a range of issues including energy, resources and pollution as well as social, economic and political aspects. The results of studies and technical information can therefore appear in a large number of journals, reports and books representing this wide range of interests. The aim of this chapter is to briefly survey some of the more important aspects of these issues, identify major literature review works and to introduce the terminology and definitions used in the secondary metals industries. A major aim of the current work is to provide a detailed account of modern technology used for the physical beneficiation of secondary metals and to provide an up-to-date summary of current practice in the metals reclamation field.

Resource conservation by the re-use, reclamation and recycling of materials has been practiced for millennia, and the recovery of metals and alloys is a prime example of such activities. It has been estimated that since the dawn of civilization until 1900 the world's cumulative production of metals was about 1 billion tonnes. By 1950 this had increased to five billion tonnes and during the 1980s alone production was 5.8 billion tonnes[1]. Such massive increases have motivated interest

1

from environmental and "green" groups, particularly during the past twenty years, and one result of pressure to reduce pollution by moderating primary consumption has been an increased level of recycling. Each extra tonne of metal recycled results in a reduction of primary production wastes of:

- Four tonnes for iron
- Two hundred tonnes for copper
- Two hundred thousand tonnes for platinum
- plus a 50-90% energy reduction[1]

In addition to the above figures there is also a reduction in the 200 to 300 millions tonnes per year of obsolete metal scrap[1,2,3].

In 1974 in the United Kingdom a government Green Paper was published called "War on Waste - a policy for reclamation", which, although it contained only a series of recommendations, led to an increased political and public interest in reclamation and recycling[4]. This was followed in 1976 by the first report of the Waste Management Advisory Council (WMAC) which recommended amongst other things that "A comprehensive waste management policy therefore should also aim, within economical and technical constraints, to avoid creating waste and to make the most efficient use of materials at all stages of a product's life"[5]. Further important influences have been the Control of Pollution Act (1974) and the Environmental Protection Act (1990) which have lead many authorities to reassess their disposal policies and consider reclamation as an alternative[3].

The recovery of materials from wastes and the recycling of materials are of increasing importance due to:

- Increased scarcity of economically viable deposits of some ores.
- The fact that longer term benefits from better utilization of

available resources are missed without recycling.

- Increased national and international efforts to conserve and control mineral prices (along the lines of OPEC with oil prices).
- Savings in imports (metals and energy).
- Increased pressure for nations to be self-sufficient in strategic commodities.
- Increased emphasis on pollution control.
- Potential disposal cost savings.
- The fact that rapidly increasing prices in many cases accentuate the virtue of using recycled rather than virgin raw materials[7,8].

It has been noted that society in general does not become alarmed about its resources until they are in short supply, and does not become concerned about the environment until it becomes uncomfortable or threatening[9].

For effective and efficient use of material resources a compromise is often needed between material conservation and energy expenditure. The 1973 energy crisis provided an impetus for many projects aimed at energy conservation, but interest seems to have declined and consumption of energy and raw materials has subsequently increased. One of the consequences of the exploitation of lower grade minerals and ores is the production of more waste and so the amount of waste to be disposed of from this source is also increased. In addition, demand for land is constantly increasing - in some areas land itself is a scarce resource. Such factors may lead to the limitation of the exploitation of not only non-renewable but also of renewable resources[3,6,10].

There have been many debates on these and related issues and some of the most pertinent observations that have been made are summarised following:

"One day it will begin to dawn on our masters that to plunder in a generation resources that have taken 350 million years to accumulate is a crime for which our descendants will never forgive us"[11] - "Modern society emphasises disposal rather than salvage and recovery, on the assumption that our resources are limitless, and hence our methods of waste treatment are even more primitive than in Man's early development: burning, burying or dumping in rivers and seas, coupled with much interest in advanced incineration and compaction techniques where disposal is the aim"[6] - "Almost too late we are awakening to the nightmare possibility of our teeming world strangling in its own excrement and garbage"[12] - "The environmental gains of increased recycling are reduced mining residuals, litter and pollution due to reduced energy demand and extension of the life of landfill sites"[2].

From these brief considerations it can be seen that recycling makes contributions in the important areas of energy, resources and pollution which are now considered:

i)Energy. True conservation means maximum employment of resources with minimum waste of both materials and energy. The average consumer is not usually concerned with problems of waste disposal, once an article has been thrown in the bin it is forgotten, yet throwing away an aluminium beverage can can waste as much energy as pouring out a half-filled can of petrol[14] (95 000 equivalent BTUs to make one pound of primary aluminium compared with 4 300 equivalent BTUs to make one pound of secondary aluminium)[15]. Table 1 illustrates clearly the energy reduction that can be achieved by the reclamation of some commonly used materials.

The energy requirement for the production of aluminium is mainly consumed in the reduction cell, and hence the total energy costs are not as dependent on the grade of the ore as for most metals. Despite this, the energy requirement for aluminium

TABLE 1.   Environmental benefits of recycling: United States*.

	Paper	*Aluminium*	*Iron and steel*
Reduction of energy use	30–55%	90–95%	60–70%
Reduction of spoil/solid waste	130%	100%	95%
Reduction of air pollution	95%	95%	30%

* percent reduction in BTU, tons of waste, tons of particulates, etc., per ton of material recycled.

extraction, from bauxite mining to final ingot, is about 300 000 MJ/tonne, compared to the energy used in producing secondary aluminium, 9 288 MJ/tonne for clippings to 17 996 MJ/tonne for old wire and cable[18]. Hence, even where reducing grades do not seriously affect overall production costs of primary materials, increasing energy costs merit a move towards greater utilisation of secondary materials.

ii)Resources. Resource thrift is the basis of any natural system – waste produced at one point in a cycle is used to good advantage in the next – "Without autumn there would be no spring"[12]. Where raw materials have been abundant it has been common practice to choose the more immediately profitable path of using virgin raw materials rather than regarding used materials as potentially valuable resources, despite the fact that the overall society value of recycling is high[3,16]. The production of easily recycled products (forming high potential value resources) is another area with high long term society value but lower immediate value to the producer. A modern trend for materials of construction has been away from metals and towards more use of polymers, ceramics and composites – and yet metals can be more easily recovered[16].

The exponential growth in the use of materials and growth in waste generation makes recycling an obvious goal[6]. Re-use, reclamation and recycling are not absolute solutions, but they can slow down exploitation of mineral resources - consumption levels of certain resources are now so high that their continued availability in the future has been questioned[3]. Recycling at the 100% level is impossible because of growth in consumption, energy limitations and physical laws, and it can only have a significant effect on depletion of non-renewable resources if high recovery rates are achieved. During periods of growth more material is consumed every year and since the materials available for recycling are the products of some years ago, recycling can only provide, assuming a constant recovery rate, a declining proportion of the total materials demand - thus, recycling cannot sustain growth in the long term[3].

There has been considerable debate in the past about whether limitations on resource availability present a real threat to contemporary society. There are extreme views on the matter, one being exemplified by a study called *Limits to Growth* (1972)[17] which was concerned with when reserves of minerals and fuels would run out. Typical data that was produced by the study is given in Table 2.

TABLE 2.   Non-renewable resource lifetimes[17].

Resource	Lifetime at current rate of consumption	Lifetime at projected rate of growth of consumption
Aluminium	100 years	31 years
Copper	36 "	21 "
Gold	11 "	9 "
Iron	240 "	93 "
Lead	26 "	21 "
Petroleum	31 "	20 "
Silver	16 "	13 "
Tin	17 "	15 "
Zinc	23 "	18 "

Critics took an opposite view and argued that the analysis used to produce such predictions was too simplified and that as any resource becomes scarcer its price increases, resulting in increased exploration for new reserves and the search for substitute materials. Thus problems of resource supply would be solved by the price mechanism drawing forth new reserves so that, in the foreseeable future, resources will not be in short supply. Time has shown that the barren future predicted in the *Limits to Growth* has not occurred (gold, iron, petroleum, silver, tin and zinc have not run out), but a viewpoint between the extremes probably represents the true case. A prudent approach to the problem of resource depletion is desirable, however, as once a natural material reserve has been depleted its use in the future must constantly decline[3]. It can be reasonably maintained that it is economic cost, rather than actual physical depletion, that will provide constraints on resource use in the future. It is likely that the only structural metals which will not be in short supply in the future are magnesium (from sea water), aluminium and iron[6].

iii)Pollution. Eventually all products are discarded. The mountains of litter discarded by both industrialized and developing countries are continually increasing. It is therefore desirable to reprocess these wastes to reclaim as much material as is possible. For material with no apparent secondary use (as a material source), such as the combustibles contained in automobile shredder rejects, energy recovery should be the aim. The recycling of waste has a double effect on both pollution and energy. For pollution it both reduces waste that has already been generated and at the same time it reduces the pollution involved in primary production of materials (solid, liquid and gaseous). For energy it can provide an extra source of raw material and also reduces the amount of energy used in primary production.

Despite the overall advantages of recycling, it will only take place where the economic incentive is great enough. Almost without exception a resource will be processed for its materials if there is sufficient financial incentive to do so under prevailing conditions[16].   Extensive recycling only occurs when economically justified and economic conditions depend on both supply and demand.   The balance is shifting as supplies dwindle and demand grows.   More and more materials now justify the expenditure of energy and effort necessary for conservation[6].

1.1   GENERAL DEFINITIONS USED IN MATERIALS RECYCLING

A number of different terms are used to describe or define materials and operations in the reclamation industries and these have been collated and listed below:

1. *By-product generation.*   Recovered materials and products used for a different purpose[8].
2. *Consumer waste.*   Urban waste (see below) plus abandoned cars and litter[6].
3. *Direct recycling.*   For example the returnable bottle.   Once a returnable bottle is unfit for re-use (see below), it may be cleaned and broken down for cullet, i.e. glass that is re-melted at the glassworks to make more bottles.   This probably applies to metals more than any other materials.   Strongly influenced by the fact that some materials degrade in quality on continued reprocessing – paper and plastics are the two major examples[19].
4. *Garbage.*   Domestic or household food waste[6].
5. *Home/in-house scrap.*   Unavoidable non-product output of industry manufacturing a material[6].
6. *Indirect recycling.*   For example the returnable bottle.   A mixture of glass colours may make cullet unsuitable for glass manufacture without costly sorting – it could, for example, be used for a highly skid resistant and durable road surfacing material.   Other examples are pyrolysis and incineration with heat recovery[19].

7. *Obsolete/old/post-consumer scrap.* Those materials that are available in products discarded by the consumer[6]

8. *Prompt scrap.* Non-product output of fabrication operations[6].

9. *Reclamation.* Collection by scrap merchants of homogeneous or mixed wastes to be sold for recycling[6]. Process of making a product regarded as waste available for further use[3].

10. *Recovery.* Collecting homogeneous wastes for re-use within a factory[6]. Separation out of materials and discards from waste[8].

11. *Recycling.* Actual process for re-using materials, either direct, indirect, or energy utilisation[6]. Recovered material used for production of more of a similar material[8].

12. *Resources.* Natural fuel and non-fuel mineral deposits and other natural entities such as forests, rivers and geothermal wells[20].

13. *Reserves.* Only that part of a resource that can be extracted and marketed economically under prevailing prices and market conditions. Thus reserves are conditional quantities dependent on national economy. Given appropriate economic conditions, they may include waste, for example municipal refuse[20].

14. *Refuse.* Solid waste[6].

15. *Re-use.* Recovered product used again for similar purpose, for example the returnable bottle[8,19]. Highest availability in the recycling system in that the least energy and process complexity is required in getting the article back into use[19].

16. *Rubbish.* Domestic non-food waste[6].

17. *Salvage.* Extraction of homogeneous waste from a mixture of wastes[6].

18. *Urban waste.* All waste collected by a local authority other than sewage, e.g. domestic waste, street and other municipal waste, and commercial (office/shop) waste[6].

19. *Waste products.* Those that the generator finds more profitable to discard than to utilize - includes agricultural, household, human and industrial wastes[21].

1.2 THE POTENTIAL FOR RESOURCE RECOVERY

The United States Department of the Interior, through the Bureau
of Mines (USBM) has probably conducted more research into resource
recovery than any other organisation.   Since it was founded in
1910, USBM has always regarded waste and scrap as resources.   It
is charged with aiding in the conservation and development of the
United States resources, and one way to conserve resources is to
re-use or recycle metals and minerals already removed from the
earth's crust.   USBM also played a major part in developing
technology to comply with the 1965 Solid Waste Disposal Act and
the 1970 Resource Recovery Act.

Present day rubbish dumps represent a mine above ground and
may in the future be mined - a practical demonstration that it is
unnecessary and perhaps inappropriate to divide secondary and
primary sources of raw materials[6,20].   Much less processing energy
is normally required to recycle the constituents of "urban ore"
than to obtain them in equal amounts from natural raw materials.
In contrast with many natural resources, urban ore is growing in
abundance, rich in grade and variety of value, and comparatively
simple to process.   It is also very costly to dispose of by
conventional methods[20,22].   Probably the biggest disadvantage of
processing urban ore is the quality of the final product due to
the difficulty of processing an heterogeneous mixture.   Many of
the materials currently recovered could be further upgraded to
replace valuable primary materials[8].

Solid waste disposal is an expensive operation, costs being
estimated at between $30-$100 per tonne.   It is possible to
achieve a 40% reduction in solid waste by recycling, and with
about one tonne of waste produced by every household per year,
this is a huge reduction, and yet only about a quarter of the
world's paper, aluminium and steel is recovered for re-use[14,23].
It should be noted that although total quantity of waste arisings
are not affected by recycling, those requiring disposal can be

significantly reduced.

In the United Kingdom, in excess of 23 million tonnes per year of municipal solid waste (MSW) is disposed of by local authorities, of which 89% is tipped, 9% incinerated, 0.5% composted and the remainder reclaimed[3,19,24,25]. Industrial conurbations tend to be the only places to use incineration, and the only materials significantly recovered are ferrous metals - despite this, about one million tonnes per year of ferrous scrap is lost per year in MSW[23,24]. In 1974 Warren Spring Laboratory estimated the total value of non-ferrous metals lost in MSW to be of the order of £39 million[26].

TABLE 3.   Metal content of UK household refuse[24].

	Quantity (tonnes/yr)	Percentage of domestic refuse
Ferrous	1 284 000	7.34%
Non-ferrous	(116 000)	(0.66%)
Aluminium	43 300	0.25%
Copper	25 400	0.15%
Nickel	500	–
Tin	7 800	0.04%
Zinc	39 000	0.22%
Total	1 400 000	8.00%

In the nine EEC countries, (in 1974), the total materials available for reclamation were 10-20 million tonnes per year of MSW (available = currently discarded as waste, not at present recovered, and not dissipated to an extent that would make recovery impractical)[8].

In the United States, between 130 and 200 million tonnes of MSW are collected each year[12,13]. In 1978 there were 14 MSW processing plants operating for the purpose of resource recovery, and a further 13 under construction, indicating that resource recovery from MSW was commercially viable. Even if a process does not make a profit, the losses incurred should be less than those involved with straightforward disposal.

1.3 SECONDARY METALS

Metals have played a unique and essential role in the development of modern society. For as long as metals have been utilized they have been recycled, for example copper has been recycled since the Bronze Age[24]. It is popular, however, to consider resource recovery technology beginning in the 1960s or, at a stretch, the 1950s, but interesting to note that Europe's metal trade was reorganized nearly 4000 years ago, to ensure more complete collection, recovery and re-utilization of bronze scrap[13].

Re-use of products was the main method of recycling - broken items were repaired wherever possible. Despite high levels of recycling, solid waste disposal was a common feature of the larger ancient cities, as population density increased and area for disposal decreased, the need for advanced disposal systems increased. Minoan solid wastes in the Cretan capital, Knossos (3000 BC) were placed in large pits with layers of earth as a covering at various levels. This was not the case in all ancient cities, however. The Romans re-used large amounts of waste but they had no organised system of waste removal-disposal and wastes accumulated in the streets and around the towns and villages. This practice persisted until the nineteenth century. A common practice in mediæval German cities was to avoid being buried in their own wastes by requiring that departing wagons which had been used to bring produce into the city return with a load of wastes to be deposited in the countryside[36].

The main methods of recycling in primitive societies were the feeding of garbage to animals; re-using containers; repairing tools; re-using timber to build ships; using rags as the raw materials for paper and organic waste for fertilizer. Labour was more readily available than materials, hence recycling was easy. With thrift and skill profitable uses could be found for virtually every kind of waste in the period up to the beginning of the industrial revolution[3,6,36].

Cementation was first practiced in Spanish copper mines during the sixteenth century (cementation on scrap iron accounted for about 10% of United States production in 1980)[13]. The growth of metals reclamation in Britain originates in the lack of raw materials on which to form a primary smelting industry[3].

Early American settlers and pioneers had to practice recycling. For instance, old buildings were burned to recover nails. The refuse yards of Edinburgh remained the same size for a century in the eighteenth and nineteenth centuries because everything which was brought in was sorted and eventually sold. Over a century ago, Dickens was writing about reclaiming values from *dust heaps* in his book *Hard Times*. That those dust heaps could be given as dowries makes a relevant point: reclamation technologies have developed in response to economic incentive[13,36].

Mechanized sorting of scrap has been practiced for at least a century as the following account of an early process shows:

"*Recovery of Brass Waste* - In order to separate mixed filings it was usual to remove the iron and steel by means of a magnet held in the hand, when the brass filings remained. Vavin, a French engineer, has constructed a machine to shorten this tedious operation. It has already been tried in practice and is made by Cail & Co. of Paris.

This machine consists of two drums, rotating on their axes, and placed one above the other. The surfaces of the drums are covered by alternate strips of soft iron and copper. Each iron strip is suitably connected with a series of horse-shoe magnets, which are so arranged that the one pole of the magnet is in contact with one iron strip, the other pole with the next. The mixture of metal filings is contained in a hopper with a vibrating foot, from which the filings fall in a stream nearly as wide as the drum.   The iron filings are attracted by the iron strips on the drum, which are made magnetic, and are carried away by them until they are swept off into a receiver by a rotating brush.   The brass filings and a portion of the mixture of the two metals fall upon the second drum, which is similar to the upper drum, but is so placed that the iron and copper strips are in such a position to those on the upper drum that strips of different metals always come into the same vertical plane.   Whilst now the brass filings fall straight off, the separating process is completed by the iron filings attached to the surface being removed by the cylindrical brush on the other side and swept into the receiver.   The machine is driven by hand or from shafting; it requires a floor space of only 2ft 6ins by 1ft 2ins and a height of 5ft 3ins."[37]

The use of the open hearth furnace for steelmaking (45% scrap feed) declined dramatically following World War II, giving way to the basic oxygen furnace (28% scrap feed).   The basic oxygen furnace produced only 4% of US steel in 1960 but by 1986 was producing over 61% - a trend that has adversely affected recycling.   The use of the electric arc furnace has grown over the same period, from 8 to 28% of US production and has had the opposite effect.   Over the world as a whole the use of the electric arc furnace has grown dramatically, especially in those countries with the highest steel recycling rates[14].

The secondary metals industries have traditionally served the purpose of re-using the mineral values contained in waste.   Just as municipal landfills can be seen as man-made mines so can scrap car graveyards - the utilization of municipal landfills rely on economies of scale because of the comparatively low metal content, whereas the automobile (and large domestic appliances) provides an extremely high grade and fairly homogeneous feedstock[27].   When shredded, 75% of the metal content of cars and domestic appliances can be completely recycled[28].

The British secondary metals industry transformed from a labour intensive industry (manual sorting and little capital equipment) in the 1950s, to a capital intensive industry by the mid 1970s[3]. This has coincided with the immense progress in auto shredding since 1960[13].

The secondary metals industries do not only recycle old scrap. The myriad of industrial processes that give final products all produce scrap. Most is generated as prompt industrial scrap and forms the basis of the secondary metals industry. In the United States alone it is worth around $5 billion per year[12,13] - the manufacturing community understands the values of its residues and practices recycling more than any other sector of the economy. Over the world as a whole, in 1985, the total crude steel production was 717 million tonnes, consuming 270 million tonnes of scrap. Of this scrap feed approximately 30-45% was home scrap, so approximately 170 million tonnes of steel scrap was purchased from the secondary metals industry[29]. The steelworks and foundries of the United Kingdom consumed approximately 7.7 million tonnes of scrap while making 18.9 million tonnes of new steel in 1988[28].

All metals can be recycled if the need is great enough, for example goldsmiths go to great lengths to recover gold dust, but supplies of metals such as tin and zinc, with reserves that may be measured in limited terms are widely dissipated as surface treatments for steels[6]. Industrial processes take a resource from a dispersed state, refine and process it with additional energy inputs and thus increase concentration. This is followed, due to product design, by combination of this concentrate with many others and distribution of the finished article throughout the country/world. Thus the resources become even more dissipated than they were originally. The combination of metals with other materials, especially in small quantities, makes recycling difficult as it is energy intensive to reverse the process and reclaim the component materials[3]. There has probably been more mixing of metals in products made in the last thirty years than ever before, and as the average life of a metal product is about 20-30 years, the problems facing secondary processors due to dissipation of metals will probably increase. The importance of the secondary metals industry to the UK economy can be judged by reference to the data given in Table 4 below:

TABLE 4.   **UK consumption of non-ferrous metals and fraction recycled**[23]

	Aluminium	*Copper*	*Lead*	*Zinc*	*Platinum*
UK consumption (tonnes)	668 000	699 000	64 000	391 000	18.7
Approximate scrap recovery as a % of consumption	26%	37%	62%	21%	58%

The choice between recovery and disposal depends on technology, economics and attitude[24].

i)*Technology*. For most materials there is at least one recovery route where the potential value of the material recovery is likely to exceed the costs involved, allowing for a saving in disposal costs[8].

The value of recoverable materials in most products is usually small in relation to the initial cost, therefore it is difficult to persuade and motivate the manufacturer and first time buyer to make any changes to the product which would improve the eventual ease of recovery of its materials of construction, especially if the changes cost money or have a small (actual or imagined) effect on the initial performance of the product[16]. Nevertheless, some progress in this area has recently been reported from the automotive industry.

The important technological aspects are state of development, availability, possible combination of processes, operational reliability, etc.[30]. Due to changing fortunes in markets, scrap tends to be used to make up feeds as a marginal - one solution to this problem is the development of technologies where scrap is the basic raw material, rather than a marginal increment in supply - electric furnaces (especially minimills)[13] provide a good example where one tonne of crude steel produced by the blast furnace/basic oxygen furnace route requires about 16 GJ using about 25% scrap, whereas a 100% scrap fed electric arc furnace requires only 8.5 GJ per tonne of crude steel - an energy saving of 56%[29].

Occasionally technical difficulties such as impurity of product mean that new uses need to be found for some products of recycling (i.e. indirect recycling) - for instance waste rubber tyres are used to produce aromatic oils and char by pyrolysis, and surfacing of sports stadia and production of moulded parts by physical processing[6,30].

ii)*Economics*. Economic considerations at present are the major criteria for recycle feasibility. However desirable it may be to reduce the drain on natural resources or to reduce pollution, it is commercial nonsense to market a reclaimed product at a higher price than its virgin equivalent[6,31]. What is often missed is the opportunity to use recycling itself as a means of disposal - an unprofitable recovery proposal may appear attractive when viewed as a disposal method - there is no practical alternative to the high cost of refuse disposal without recycling. Energy and materials recovery systems are more than competitive with low pollution incinerators[20,24,32].

Very often in the past the analysis of the potential of waste as a raw material source has been in a physical-technological context rather than an economic one. The problems of acquisition, collection, cost of processing and transport of the output raw material have tended to be overlooked. Collection, transport, and transfer account frequently for 60-80% of the total costs - hence it is most desirable to have a large mass of high quality material close to the source of production and also to have the market close to the source of production[8,30,33].

Raw materials of mineral origin comprise the most vital ingredients for building or maintaining the economy of any industrialized nation. The wealth and economy of the entire industrialized world are determined primarily by the availability of mineral resources. No industrial nation can develop and maintain economic growth without a continuous and adequate supply of raw materials of mineral origin, so it is financially advantageous for materials to be directly recycled wherever possible, rather than used as fuel or compost, since their value as a substitute for a primary material is higher than as a by-product[8,20].

Britain is heavily dependent on many essential raw materials imports, almost wholly dependent on imports for supplies of primary non-ferrous ores for example, and the loss of potentially valuable raw materials to the waste stream is particularly serious - the total import bill for new raw materials is of the order of several thousands of millions of pounds sterling per year[3,23].

Total scrap demand for the world has remained relatively constant over recent years, but the amount of purchased scrap and associated contaminants has increased because of a fall in home scrap, due to technical processing advances such as continuous casting. A shortage of scrap is not in sight but good quality scrap may become scarcer and more expensive[29].

Secondary metals tend to be at a premium during peak economic activity due to high demand for materials and there are severe fluctuations in price and demand. This is probably the biggest economic problem in scrap processing - a smooth economic pattern does not exist. Scrap is very vulnerable to market fluctuations as it is only a marginal[8,13]. A good example is the volatility of the price of steel scrap - when there is an upswing phase in the steel cycle, scrap is used to raise production quickly; when there is a downswing; consumption of scrap is decreased because hot metal is preferred to avoid the idling of blast furnaces. This leads to speculative stocking and de-stocking which further influences the situation[29].

Export barriers have been erected specifically to reduce the price of scrap metal - a measure that reduces the incentive to collect scrap and makes it less available as a substitute for primary materials. The greatest impediment to the use of scrap in developing countries is the practice of richer countries restricting scrap exports[14]. For instance in 1989 the United States saw large increases of stainless steel scrap used domestically but exports decreased by a similar amount[34].

The capital required for secondary plants tends to be less than that required for primary plants of the same capacity - a scrap based steel plant requires about one third of the investment required for a fully integrated iron and steel plant[29].

iii)*Attitude.* The effect of attitude of consumers towards secondary materials cannot be overstated. Users tend to prefer primary materials, usually unnecessarily. Prejudice, stigma, politics, apathy, and self-interest all affect the marketability of secondary resources. Recycled materials tend to be regarded merely as a stop-gap solution to shortages of primary materials, rather than an alternative and possibly cheaper source of supply.

A recurrent theme that has emerged in the literature from those engaged in technical, economic and social aspects of the recycling industries can be summarized by the general statement: "If more people can be encouraged to regard wastes as valuable resources..."[8,23,24].

1.4 RANKING OF SCRAP

Scrap can be categorized into three main classes; home scrap, new scrap and old scrap and these classes have been ranked according to the diagram given as Figure 1 below[35].

	Home scrap	*New scrap*	*Old scrap*
Quality	←		
Time lag			→
Intensity of recycling	←		

FIGURE 1.   Typical ranking of the three classes of scrap.   The arrows indicate the direction of increase.

New scrap has the most desirable characteristics (other than home scrap):

- It is of known chemical composition.
- There are few, if any, unpleasant surprises.
- Generally in a metallic state which offers energy conservation over processing primary materials.
- Capital costs for same capacity smelters are cheaper for secondary than primary processes[13].

Recovery of potentially valuable materials from the solid waste stream is much more difficult than the recovery of homogeneous, uncontaminated manufacturing scrap[12,21]. A high proportion of materials available for reclamation arise as a part of mixed waste - it is therefore desirable to minimise mixing or dilution - for example by separation at source[6,8].

Complexity of product may make it difficult to separate different metals and alloys and contamination resulting from incomplete separation is a cause for concern to the metals industries, most of which use some recycled materials. Contamination could also have adverse effects on the purchaser of a recycled product - for example a build up of cadmium in reclaimed copper might leach out into drinking water, etc. During the past forty years the range of metals and alloys in use has greatly expanded and this has led to problems of identifying and segregating alloys present in mixed waste streams[2,6].

Although there are other factors, it is the unpredictable quality of some secondary materials that may make then unacceptable for some applications. However, there are usually less demanding alternative applications for which they may be used[16].

1.5 THE POTENTIAL FOR IMPROVED PROCESSING

In the automobile area, progress since 1960 has been exceptional. Scrap automobile recycling is at 90% with the widespread use of shredding technology which has improved the quality of ferrous scrap to the steelmaker. Similarly, there have been technical advances in the reclamation of non-ferrous metals, for example the Huron Valley Steel Corporation introduced a sink-float plant to treat non-ferrous metals from shredders in 1970 and by 1978 it was recovering 25 000 tonnes per year *each* of zinc and aluminium.

Despite the above, and other successes, such as the development of non-ferrous eddy current separators, the technical problems in the obsolete scrap area are significant. Separation should be made more efficient so that greater amounts of purer, more valuable materials can be obtained. Products should be designed with a view to recycling in order to make the process easier and cheaper. There should be economic optimisation of alternative recycling technologies[13,24].

At present the secondary metals industries rely almost exclusively on traditional pyrometallurgy for separation and purification. Low energy processes should be used where possible. If physical separation is possible then it is preferable to chemical separation which usually requires large inputs of energy, chemicals and technology.

CHAPTER TWO

UNIT OPERATIONS IN SECONDARY METALS PROCESSING

Before a metal can be processed for recycling it is usually
necessary to separate it from a variety of other materials. This
separation always requires the expenditure of energy as it opposes
the natural tendency to increasing disorder. Materials have many
unique physical and chemical properties which may be applied in
separation processes, ranging from colour, density, and texture
utilized subconsciously in manual sorting, to magnetic and
electrical properties which require mechanical equipment[6].

In most cases the cost of sorting is relatively high. The
salvage industry in the past has been based primarily on
reclaiming waste from commercial industrial operations that yield
large, clean batches. At the other end of the scale, valuable
materials may not be utilized to any great extent because of low
concentrations[6].

Any sorting operation involves a prior identification/coding
step. In some cases this is a single, unique, physical property –
for example in the magnetic separation of ferrous from non-ferrous
metals. In other cases it is necessary to deal with
multicomponent items – for example a can with tinned steel body,
aluminium ends and a paper label. Here there are two
possibilities. Use several sensors observing and measuring
physical properties (as a human sorter would) to come to a
conclusion about the nature of the item – or grind or shred
everything so finely that most of the individual particles are
homogeneous, and then separate. This second alternative has the
disadvantage that the "order" and concentration of material that

23

already exists is destroyed, although the product, after separation, is more homogeneous and probably in a physical form that is easier to handle[6].

2.1 COMMINUTION

Size reduction is subsidiary to separation but is generally essential in order that the valuable material may be liberated from the gangue for efficient separation.   Individual particles can then be coded and separated from each other.   The size of separating equipment need not be as large after size reduction - for example the cross-section of an elutriator for subsequent processing may be reduced[6].

Most separation equipment is designed to treat material showing homogeneity in physical characteristics, for example the mineral jig is designed to separate materials of different specific gravity but similar particle size (i.e. narrow size range), this is so that the separation unit operation is as efficient as possible.   The mineral processing industry has saved large amounts of time and money by employing grinding followed by sizing prior to the application of the jig[12].   In the processing of MSW the efficiency of magnetic separation without shredding is 50%, but with shredding this is increased to 90%[19].

Size reduction is carried out on MSW by impacting, shearing, grinding, milling, pulverizing, shredding or flailing.   The term "shredding" is most commonly used to describe these operations whether the action is grinding or impaction, and the name "shredder" is used generally to denote any size reduction equipment used in resource recovery, a definition not universally accepted, especially in the mining/minerals industry[6,38].

Shredders come in many different shapes and sizes, but basically consist of a rotor with arms or hammers which impact the refuse against fixed grates, bars or anvils.   The degree of size reduction and liberation obtained is a function of design - mainly grate bar spacing and hammer speed, and the power required is a function of composition of feed, mean particle size and geometry of the shredder[19].

The most efficient application of force to a material to reduce its size is that which causes the minimum expenditure of work energy. The minerals processing industry has long known of the inefficiency of size reduction operations, and shredders are no exception, only about 1% of the work input is usefully used in size reduction. For material size reduction tensile, compressive, or shearing forces could be employed. The mixed characteristics of refuse pieces and particles in MSW mean that the application of shearing forces, on average, will result in the minimum expenditure of energy, i.e. the minimum input of work to effect the desired size reduction. This is the reason for the predominance of hammermills in size reduction of mixed solid wastes[12,38]. Calculations of efficiency, performance, power, etc. can be found in *Unit Operations in Resource Recovery Engineering*[38].

Hammermills. Hammermills are the most widespread comminution devices used for resource recovery (see Figure 2). They consist of single or multiple rotor axles with attached hammers as shown in Figure 3. The hammers can be either rigid or flexible, and the whole rotor is enclosed in a heavy duty housing. The rotor swings the hammers in an arc and into contact with the material to be reduced. Fixed blocks or obstacles are positioned on the inner surface of a cylinder to provide the necessary reaction for shredding the material, or plates are positioned on the inside of the cylinder, so that material is caught between the swinging hammers and the wall, with small tolerance. There are many variations, in one the hammers approach the input area for the feed in an upswing manner, so that the material that is not easily reduced is rejected by the hammers and knocked back into a reject chute. There are horizontal hammermills, where the rotor is

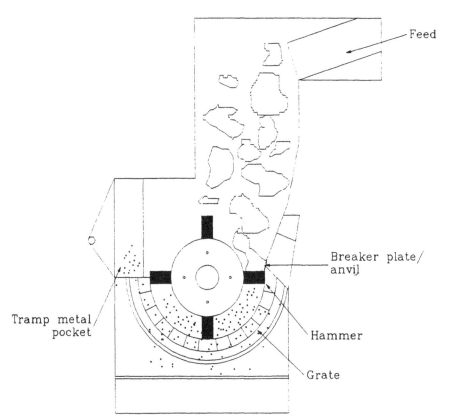

FIGURE 2.   Schematic diagram of a hammermill

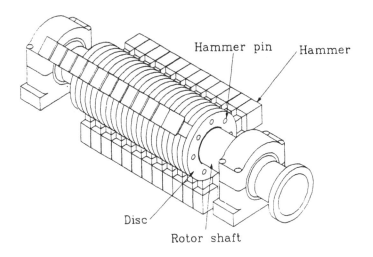

FIGURE 3.   Horizontal shredder (internal)

supported by bearings on either end, which are gravity or conveyor fed, and where the discharge plate determines the size of the product, and vertical hammermills, which consist of a vertical shaft, where gravity brings material down the sides of the housing, into an ever decreasing clearance (Figure 4)[12,38].

Flail mills. These are horizontal axis units, with lightweight hammers, blades or chains mounted on single rotor or dual opposing rotor shafts. They are used where the small particle size of the hammermill is not needed. Typical operating conditions are about 800-1500 rpm and 75-300 kW[39].

Disc mills and wet pulpers. A disc mill consists of a single rotating disc and a fixed surface, or two contra-rotating high speed discs. The feed material is subjected to repetitive impact between the two discs. Wet pulpers are similar in operation but they use a wet feed (10% solid slurry) rather than a dry feed[12].

Rasp mills. These are most commonly used in composting operations and are similar to pulverizers. They consist of a vertical shaft with heavy rasping arms attached which rotate at about 5-6 rpm. Rasping pins and holes, approximately 2" diameter, are peppered around the base of the mill and the rasping arms move over these, reducing the material (Figure 5)[12].

Roll crushers. See Figure 6. Malleable items pass through and are flattened, hence their apparent size increases, whereas brittle items are crushed and their particle size decreases, and subsequent separation can be effected by use of a screen[40].

Shredders and chippers. There are several designs of shredders, one has toothed wheels which rotate at different speeds, through which the waste must pass - the wheels penetrate, shear and shred the solid waste. Shredders are more generally applicable to reduction of ductile materials or materials comprised of elongated fibres, such as paper. Chippers are used for reduction of wood waste[12].

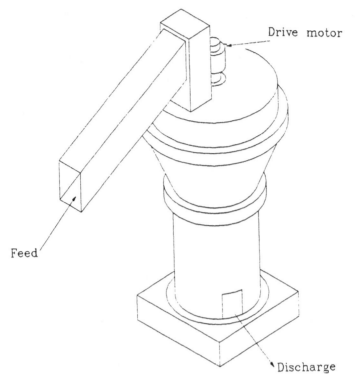

FIGURE 4.   Vertical shredder

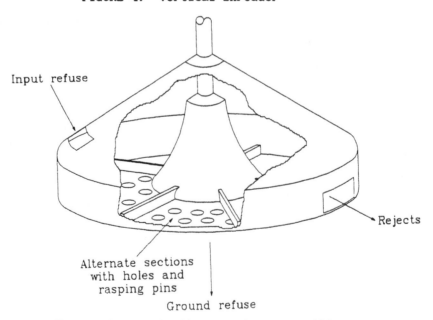

FIGURE 5.   Schematic diagram of a rasp mill

Automobile shredders (fragmentizers).   These have been developed from the tin can shredder from the Second World War, and are based on the hammermill.   They are large high power input units with high capital cost, but since 1960 have revolutionized scrap processing[12].   Autoshredders come in many sizes, and are constantly being developed to take more and more difficult feeds such as No. 2 scrap and some No. 1 scrap.   There are two methods for dealing with this type of feed, which is too heavy for the normal shredder and too light for the shear.   The first is to toughen up the whole shredder, so that it can handle heavier items (as practiced by Newell Industries), and the second is to use a system   such   as   the   Lindemann   Kondirator,   which   rejects unshreddable items automatically by running backwards, i.e. reverse rotation on the rotor.   Lindemann also produce a *Super Heavy Duty* shredder of their own design as do Hammermills Inc. [41,42].

The Newell Industries Super Heavy Duty damp/wet Shredder.   This can handle 120-180 tons per hour of scrap metals, including:

- Complete cars with or without engines in "as received" or flattened condition;
- Pressed and sheared light iron compacted to no more than 65 lb/ft^3 (1 t/m^3);
- "White Goods", i.e. household appliances, washing machines, refrigerators, etc.;
- Light iron scrap normally classified as No. 2 heavy melting material, foundry grades of scrap and some grades normally classified as No. 1 heavy melting material except unshreddable items[41].

Examples of unshreddable items (for this shredder) have been supplied by the manufacturer of the equipment and these are reproduced in the following list:

- 1" (25 mm) cable in more than 50' (15 m) sections;
- Alloy shaft in excess of 2" (50 mm);
- Mild steel shafting in excess of 2¼" (63 mm);
- Plate greater than 1" (25 mm) thick that is more than 1' (300 mm) in any direction;
- Plate more than 2" (50 mm) thick that is greater than 6" (150 mm) in any direction;
- Structural shapes of more than ¼" (6 mm) sections;
- Re-bar more than 2" in diameter;
- High carbon bars more than 1" (25 mm) in diameter;
- Truck axles rated in excess of 14 000 lbs (6 tons) for front axles and 38 000 lbs (17 tons) for rear axles;
- Ingots, billets and similar types of material.

This list is not exhaustive[41].

The shredder is designed so that unshreddable items will not normally damage the shredder. It is essential to remove containers that may contain inflammable/explosive materials (e.g. fuel tanks). Unshreddables are rejected through a door in the upper section[41].

The ferrous product conforms to industry specification for fragmentized scrap, with a range of sizes/density, from 60 to 110 lbs/ft^3 (0.9-1.6 t/m^3). The shredder will also shred non-ferrous scrap, swarf (turnings), industrial waste, foundry waste, etc. The shredder is rated at 6000 HP (4470 kW), 600 rpm, at 6000 volts (three phase, 50 Hz supply)[41]. USBM used a Newell shredder in its research into autoshredding with the following rating: 2000 HP Newell hammermill, with 16 double faced 250 lb swing hammers; 730 rpm, processing 250 tons/day (31 autos per hour)[43].

The Newell Industries Megashredder. This was developed following the success of the *Newell Super Heavy Duty Shredder*. With a motor power of 6000 HP it can process up to 300 tons/hour and can process a heavier grade scrap more easily than the largest commonly operated shredders. It is fed by a new development in shredder technology - a smart *Newell Super Double Feed Roll* which uses programmable logic control to feed the shredder at the ideal rate. This technology has been developed so that it can be fitted to other shredders[43].

The Lindemann Zerdirator is a standard shredder which can accept light mixed scrap, scrap cans, pressed and sheared, flattened cars, computer scrap, refuse reclaimed materials, aluminium scrap, ferrous or non-ferrous swarf or drosses. The clean final product can have a density from 1.0-2.0 t/m^3, and is suitable for steelworks. The largest Zerdirator is a 6000 HP unit, with a capacity of 150-200 tons per hour of iron product from car bodies and mixed scrap, and the smallest is a 500 HP unit, with a capacity of 5-9 tons per hour of flattened cars, or 4-6 tons per hour of aluminium mixed alloys, or 10-14 tons per hour of aluminium castings (see Figure 7)[44].

There are many other types of comminution equipment used by salvage firms such as tyre shredders, cable strippers/granulators, etc. These will be discussed later.

All size reduction equipment, especially impact type machines, are subject to heavy abrasion and require regular maintenance. Both wear and energy consumption can be reduced by removal of fine materials, predominantly glass and hardened steel ball bearings, by screening before size reduction[39].

2.1.1 THERMAL TREATMENTS TO AID COMMINUTION

Selective cryogenic embrittlement. When rubber tyres are cooled to $-60°C$ in liquid nitrogen and passed through a hammermill a granular product of rubber crumb is produced, and destruction of the tyres consumes less power than it would have without pre-treatment. The crumb has a variety of uses including sports surfaces and carpet underlay. High grade scrap steel and fibre

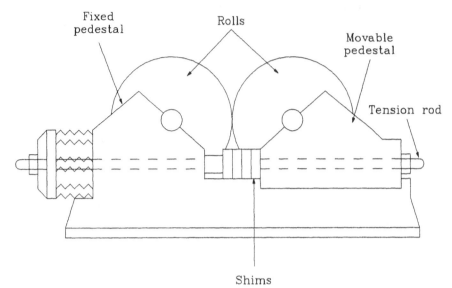

FIGURE 6.   Schematic diagram of a rolls crusher

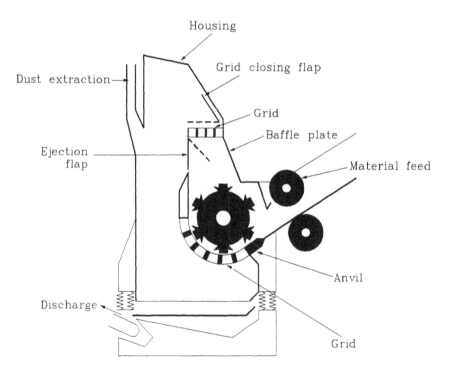

FIGURE 7.   The Lindemann Zerdirator

TABLE 5.   Size reduction equipment and potential applications to MSW[12,24]. (See also Figures 8, 9 and Tables 6, 7)

Basic types	Variations	Potential application to MSW
Crushers	Impact	Direct application as a form of hammermill.
	Jaw, roll and gyrating	As a primary or parallel operation on brittle or friable material.
Cage disintegrators	Multi-cage or single-cage	As a parallel operation on brittle, friable or disentangled material.
Shears	Multi-blade or single blade	As a primary operation on wood or ductile materials.
Shredders, cutters and clippers	Pierce-and-tear type	Direct as hammermill with meshing shredding members, or parallel on paper/box board.
	Cutting type	Parallel on paper, plastics, etc.
Rasp mills and drum pulverizers		Direct on damp MSW; bulky item sorter on parallel lines.
Disk mills/wet pulpers	Single or multiple disk	Parallel on MSW fractions for special treatment; secondary operation on pulpable material.
Hammermills		Direct application or in tandem with other types.
Grinding mills	Ball and rod	Fine grinding.

fluff are also produced. The same technique can be applied to cans, plastics and insulated copper and aluminium wire - after embrittlement, insulation and coatings are easily separated from the wire. The important properties here are the ductile-brittle transition temperature for metals and the glass transition temperature of polymers:

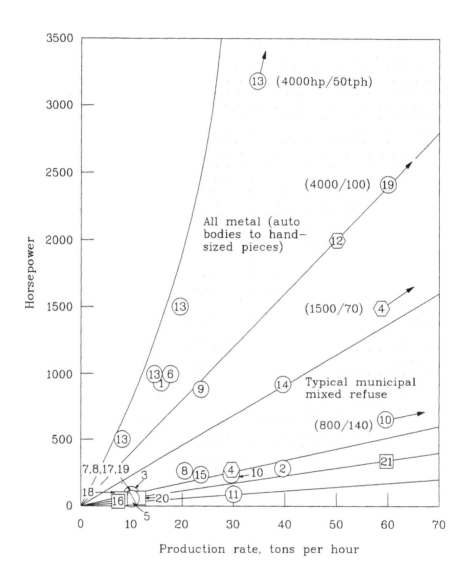

FIGURE 8.   Size reduction power requirements

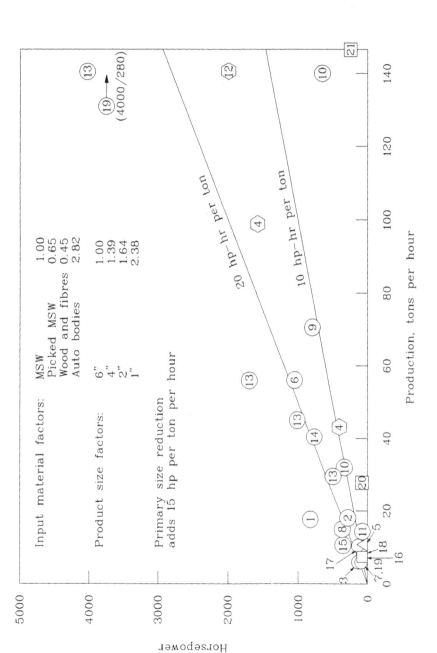

FIGURE 9. Adjusted power requirements for size reduction

Capacity[b] (Tons per hr)	Nominal product size (in.)	Costs (dollars per ton)					Variations from Packer-Truck input
		Maintenance	Equivalent annual cost	Power	Labour	Total	
17	6	0.22	0.12	0.45	0.25	1.04	Bulky waste included.
40	6	0.05	0.22	0.08	0.11	0.46	Wood only (non-bulky).
10	6	0.27	0.19	0.19	0.41	1.06	12 percent pre-picked.
30	4	0.27	0.20	0.18	0.17	0.82	Some bulky extras; 4-in. product.
9	2	0.06	0.33	0.09	0.48	0.96	30 percent durable bulky items rejected.
10	6	0.18	0.18	0.15	0.43	0.94	
7.2	4	0.25	0.25	0.21	0.61	1.32	10 percent reject of durable items.
6.1	2	0.28	0.29	0.25	0.72	1.54	
25	6	0.55	0.14	0.32	0.18	1.19	Bulky waste included.
30	6	0.55	0.17	0.10	0.14	0.96	Harbour waste.
50	6	1.10	0.18	0.40	0.09	1.77	Auto bodies.
40	6	0.55	0.09	0.20	0.11	0.95	Bulky waste included.
12	1	0.11	0.08	0.13	0.36	0.68	Pre-milled input.
60	1	0.11	0.08	0.06	0.08	0.33	Pre-milled input.

[a]These costs are based on manufacturers' data modified by users' data and do not include site costs, crane costs, or other handling costs.

[b]Tons per year = average tons per hr x 8 x 286.

TABLE 6.   Approximate size reduction costs

Horsepower	Capital investment (thousands of dollars)	Adjusted capacity (tons per hr)	Adjusted power requirements (hp-hr per ton)[a]	Adjusted unit capital investments (dollars per ton-per-hr capacity)
800	35.0	17 x 1 = 17	47	2,060
300	8.5	40 x 0.43 = 17	19	500
200	33	10 x 0.65 = 6.5	31	5,080
350	80	30 x 1.39 = 42	8.3	1,900
1,500	130	70 x 1.39 = 97	15.5	1,340
80	50	9 x 0.65 x 1.64 = 10	8.0	5,000
1,000		20 x 2.8 = 56	17.8	–
150	30	10 x 0.65 = 6.5	23	4,620
350		20 x 0.65 = 13	27	–
800	60	25 x 2.8 = 70	11.4	857
300	86	30 x 1 = 30	10	2,870
800	160	140 x 1 = 140	5.7	1,140
150	17.5	30 x 0.43 = 13	11.5	1,310
2,000	150	50 x 2.8 = 140	14.3	1,070
500		10 x 2.8 = 28	17.9	7,150
1,000	200	16 x 2.8 = 45	22	4,450
1,500		20 x 2.8 = 56	27	3,570
4,000		50 x 2.8 = 140	29	1,430
800	59.5	40 x 1 = 40	20	1,490
300	14.2	24 x 0.43 = 10	30	1,420
50	–	7 x 0.65 x 1.64 = 7.5	6	–
150	53.0	10 x 1 = 10	15	5,300
60	–	8 x 0.65 x 1.64 = 8.5	7	–
150	10	10 x 0.65 = 6.5	23	1,540
4,000	–	100 x 2.8 = 280	14	–
150 + (12 x 15) = 330	15.0	12 x 2.38 = 28.56	11.8	536
350 + (60 x 15) = 1,250	69.5	60 x 2.38 = 143	8.8	485

[a]Primary size-reduction power added.

TABLE 7. Adjusted performance and cost data for size reduction equipment.

-30°C for zinc-base die cast alloys

-40°C for poly(vinylchloride)-neoprene insulation

-60°C for poly(vinylchloride)-fabric insulation[6]

There are alternatives to liquid nitrogen such as mixtures of acetone or methanol with dry ice[6].

At -120°C iron is much more brittle than aluminium and copper and it is therefore possible to shred pre-cooled mixed metals to give very small iron flakes to separate by screening. Baled car bodies and other mixed metal scrap can thus give high quality scrap yield (99% iron). The first pilot plant using this technology was built in Liege, Belgium (1971) and is known as the *INCHSCRAP* process[6].

The *INCH* process (InterNational Centre for High quality scrap) was developed by George et Cie, the main scrap processor in Liege. Bales are cooled to -7°C by cold nitrogen at the beginning of an insulated tunnel. At the end they are immersed in a liquid nitrogen bath where their temperature reaches -120°C. Each bale is passed to a hammermill where it is reduced to coin-sized pieces in less than one minute. The liquid nitrogen consumption is 0.3 litres per kg of steel scrap produced. It has several advantages:

- High purity steel scrap - no entrainment of non-ferrous materials in magnetic scrap;
- Lower capital and operating cost for shredder (500 HP shredder with cryogenic embrittlement is equivalent to a 5000 HP shredder without);
- Increased safety - the nitrogen atmosphere in the shredder gives reduced risk of explosion;
- Easier to remove the non-ferrous metals from the non-magnetic residue[43].

This technique is particularly suitable for recovery of copper from small electric motors. USBM research has concluded that selective cryogenic embrittlement can give nearly complete separation of copper and insulation from scrap wire and good separation of zinc from copper and aluminium components of non-ferrous autoshredder residues (at -65°C)[6,43].

Thermally assisted liberation. Another feed preparation method for comminution is Thermally Assisted Liberation (TAL). Work has been conducted into the separation of copper from copper/plastic electrical scrap. The results of differential thermal analysis, mechanical strength tests and grindability determinations have shown that improved metal-plastic liberation can be achieved by subjecting the material to relatively low temperature heating and air quenching prior to milling and screening[45].

2.2 PHYSICAL SEPARATION METHODS

All the following separation devices are based on a principle of coding and separation. Some property of the material is used as a recognition code, such as magnetic/non-magnetic or large/small. At times the material has to be further coded, such as in froth flotation when conditioning agents are added which allow for the selective attachment of air bubbles to achieve a light/heavy code[38].

Once coded, the material is separated according to the code. In screening, for example, the small particles fall through the screen and the large ones are retained on the screen. First there must be a recognizable code to differentiate the materials in question, and then this code must be used in a separation device[38].

Most of the present techniques are binary coding/separation devices, with a few producing more than two classes of product. Eventually it is desirable to have coding and separating devices that will be able to identify any specific item from any other, such as an aluminium can from a plastic bottle and a china cup[38].

Hand sorting, although labour intensive, is still very widely used but more and more operations are being developed which will eventually replace hand sorting. Some doubt exists between the virtues of wet and dry processing. Dry operation, especially in Europe, tends to be preferred due to the dirty water cleaning/disposal problem[2], but wet operation removes the need for air cleaning plant and reduces the explosion risk in shredders which can then be fitted with water sprays, and it has been proposed that eventually wet processing will become dominant because of the explosion problem and air pollution problems[46].

2.2.1 HAND SORTING

Although labour intensive and costly, hand sorting is still very widely used in the reclamation industries. Applications range from "totting" and hand-picking domestic refuse, removal of "pernicious contraries" from paper prior to pulping and textile sorting to highly skilled operations in the sorting of metal scrap by alloy composition, where use is made of simple physical and chemical tests for identification[31].

For the most part, however, hand sorting is not very satisfactory and should find less acceptance in the future for a number of reasons. The first is that the factor of human error is always present in hand sorting salvage operations. In some cases, a very high purity is desired or necessary in recycled material in order to have a guaranteed resale price. Even an infrequent error in hand sorting may destroy the acceptance and marketability of salvaged materials if subsequent manufacture using the resalvaged materials is prevented or damaged because of the occasional impurity which escapes the hand sorters[12].

The second factor which limits hand sorting is the limited ability of hand sorters to separate materials of various sizes, the process tends to be limited to particles greater than 10 mm[12].

The third factor is limited output or recovery - if every item is to be sorted on a picking conveyor then the throughput will be low, and vice-versa.

The fourth factor is the low unit prices paid for salvaged materials - these tend to preclude highly labour intensive sorting operations, even if sorters are only receiving a minimum wage[12].

2.2.2 SEPARATION BY PARTICLE SIZE

Screening is the simplest means of separating a waste fraction by size and has become an increasingly important unit process in resource recovery facilities. There is a wide range of equipment available, such as flat deck vibrating screens, rotary trommel screens, rotating disc screens, sifting screens, grizzly screens, etc.[12,24,39,46]

A particle can pass a screen if it is smaller than the opening in at least two dimensions. The size differences produced between different materials after a given milling operation mean that a combination of a milling operation and a screening separation stage may be made to selectively separate various materials from the waste stream[12,38]. For instance one study[47] obtained the following results:

- 70% of glass particles produced in a hammermilling operation were smaller than $\frac{1}{16}"$ in maximum dimension.
- 60% of metal particles produced in the same milling operation were larger than 2" in least dimension.

The advantage of using screening as a pre-concentration step has also been shown in research carried out by USBM into sorting non-magnetic autoshredder rejects. Metals accounted for 82% of the plus 4 mm fraction, but only 35% of the minus 4 mm fraction[43,48].

Screens are primarily used in MSW facilities at the end of a process for glass recovery, because by then most of the glass would have been crushed to very fine particles. They are also useful in reclaiming the garbage fraction from shredded waste and as initial rough sorters at the beginning of most facilities. Early removal of glass is highly beneficial in reducing wear on downstream shredders.

Trommels. The trommel is the most popular type of screen used in salvaging operations. It is a revolving screen which consists of an inclined cylinder, mounted on rollers, with holes in the side (see Figure 10). The drum rotates at about 10-15 RPM, thus using very little power. The main advantage is resistance to blinding, most hole blockages drop off in the end. They are used widely in the scrap metals industries and are used as primary separators to concentrate metals and glass in the undersize fraction of MSW in various plants[38,39].

Shaking screens. Shaking screens have a reciprocating movement mechanically induced in the horizontal direction and are mounted either horizontally or with a gentle slope. They operate at speeds in the range of 60-800 strokes per minute and find their greatest use as grading screens for feeds down to about 12 mm. They are readily plugged by rags, etc. and abrasive materials can cause problems (Figure 11)[38,49].

Vibrating screens. The main application of vibrating screens is in crushing circuits in the minerals industry, where they are required to handle material ranging from 250 mm to 5 mm in size. This size range is ideal for the salvage industries as well (the actual range of vibrating screens goes as low as 250 μm). Vibration is induced vertically either by the rotation of a mechanical reciprocating device applied to the casing, or by electrical devices operating directly on the screen[12,49].

Grizzlies. Very coarse material is usually screened on a grizzly which, in it simplest form, consists of a series of heavy parallel

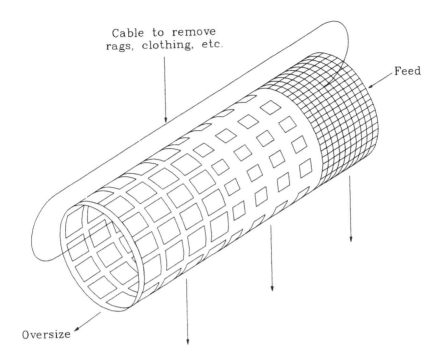

FIGURE 10.   Rotary screen or trommel

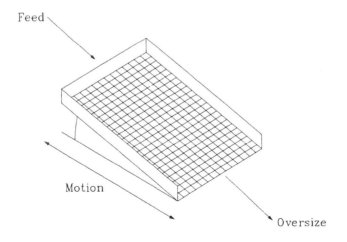

FIGURE 11.   Schematic diagram of a shaking screen

bars set in a frame.   Some grizzlies are shaken or vibrated mechanically to help the sizing and aid the removal of oversize[49].

Warren Spring Laboratory (WSL - Stevenage, England) conducted experimental work using a vibrating rod grizzly to size fragmentizer residues.   The grizzly used was a Mögensen Sizers Divergator (Figures 12, 13) set at 13.2 mm.   The work showed that no blinding occurred from bulk fragmentizer wastes, and that it was beneficial to install a vibrating rod grizzly at the front end of a metal recovery circuit, whether subsequent recovery is by mechanical or hand sorting[46].

Detailed descriptions on the operation of screens and their use can be found in *Mineral Processing Technology*[49] and *Unit Operations in Resource Recovery Engineering*[38].

2.2.3 SEPARATION BY DENSITY DIFFERENCE

There are a variety of methods utilizing differences in the specific gravity of the components of refuse to achieve separation.   These are designed to separate the "heavier" materials from the "light" materials.

2.2.3.1 Air classification

Air classification is known under several other names, such as air elutriation, winnowing and windsifting.

Classification is a method of separating mixtures of solids into two or more products on the basis of the velocity with which the grains fall through a fluid medium, such as air or water[49].

Classifiers essentially consist of a "sorting column" in which a fluid is rising at a uniform rate.   Particles either sink or rise according to whether their terminal velocities are greater or less than the upward velocity of the fluid.   The column therefore separates the feed into two products, an overflow consisting of particles with terminal velocities less than the

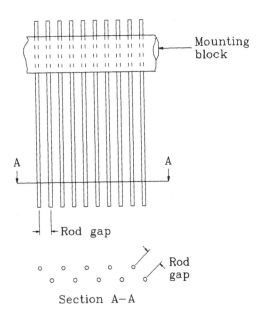

Section A—A

FIGURE 12.   View on Divergator screening surface

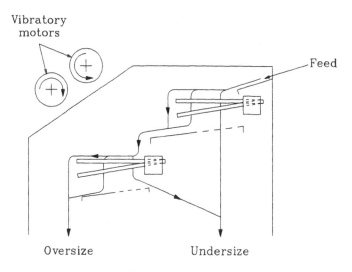

FIGURE 13.   Divergator assembly

velocity of the fluid and an underflow or spigot product of particles with terminal velocities greater than the rising velocity.   At coarser size ranges, such as those typically employed in salvage operations, the density difference has easily the most pronounced effect on classification[49].

Air classifiers are simple and efficient, and can be utilized on a wide variety of feeds.   The particles must flow in a granular manner, so fibrous materials have to be shredded.   Dust free operation can be obtained from this form of dry processing by use of air cleaning plant or closed circuit air systems.   Air classification has low capital and operating costs.   USBM estimated that the addition of an air classifier for separation of heavy materials from the output of a refuse shredder could be accomplished easily and at a cost of only 10 c per ton[3].

One of the original uses of air classifiers was to separate peanuts from their husks.   They are also used for the separation of paper labels from glass and light materials from autoshredder residue[31].   It is desirable for materials not to come into contact with the fan, so any system should either blow or have a cyclone and/or bagplant between the separating column and the fan.

Vertical air classifiers.   There are two methods of feed input into vertical air classifiers – feed is either added near to the top of the air elutriating column, or shredded refuse on a belt conveyor is subjected to an upward blast of air which entrains the paper and plastics and allows the heavies, such as metal and glass, to fall down (Figure 14).   A blower pulls the lights upwards into a separation chamber and the heavies are discharged onto a conveyor belt[19].

USBM developed a vertical classifier for use on non-magnetic autoshredder rejects and urban refuse (Figure 15)[50] with a feed point near to the top of the elutriating column.   It was used for preliminary separation of shredded refuse, or to process the middle fraction of a horizontal air separator[19].

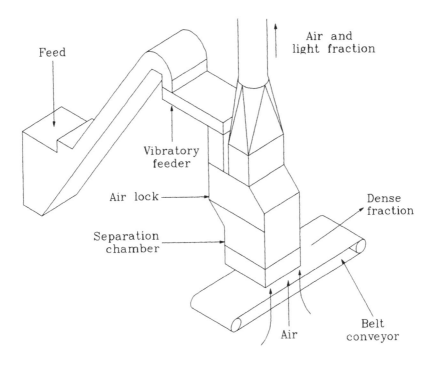

FIGURE 14. Pneumatic vertical air separator

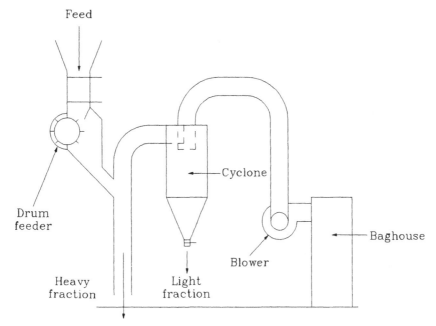

FIGURE 15. Vertical air classifier

Zigzag air classifiers. Turbulence and shear forces are required to break up flocs of particles and thus give cleaner separation - so zigzag air classifiers were introduced as a development of vertical air classifiers (Figure 16). For zigzag classifiers the largest particles in the feed should be no greater than three quarters of the diameter of the zigzag chamber[3,12,24,38].

Horizontal air classifiers. An alternative to the vertical classifier, which uses entrainment only to separate the light materials, is to use a horizontal air classifier which uses both inertia and entrainment (Figure 17). The blower is used to both "pull" and "push" - the push entrains refuse and the pull deflects it in an horizontal plane. This type of classifier can be used to sort materials into several grades and because it uses recirculating air there is no need for large scale air cleaning plants[19].

Air knives. These are basically the same as the horizontal air classifier (Figures 18, 19, 20). Air knives are probably the best air classifiers for processing fragmentizer residues (3 HP fan in comparison to a 200 HP fan of an equivalent, different design)[51].

Vibrating air classifiers. These combine the separation due to the vibration with air entrainment. The feed vibrates along a sloping surface, with the light materials shaken to the top, where the air stream carries it around in a U-shaped curve (Figure 21)[38].

Rotary air classifiers. Rotary air classifiers combine the action of a trommel screen with air entrainment (Figure 22). As the drum rotates, the aerodynamically light fraction is suspended in the air stream and carried up into a collection hopper. Small, heavy solids fall through the holes while large heavy particles exit at the lower end of the drum. A variation on this is the *Bulldog* metal cleaning system developed by Hammermills Inc. A 100 HP fan creates a suction through a rotary drum which agitates the material[52].

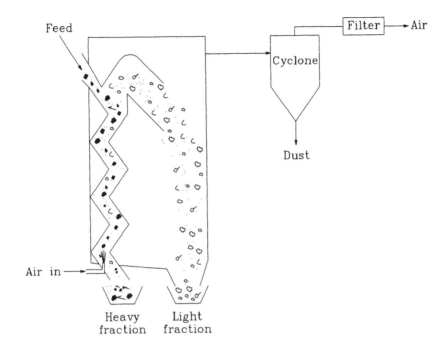

FIGURE 16. Zigzag air classifier

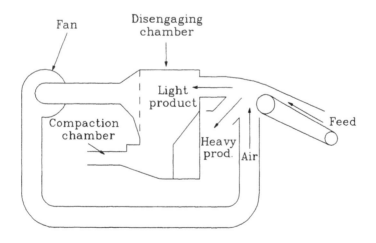

FIGURE 17. Horizontal air classifier

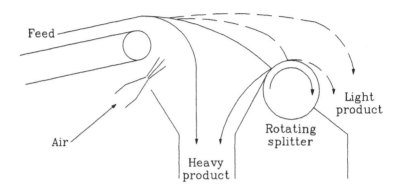

FIGURE 18.   Schematic diagram of an air knife (1)

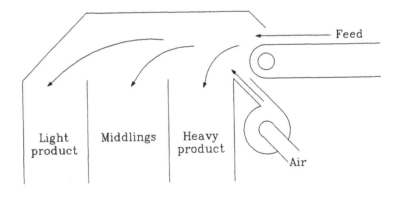

FIGURE 19.   Schematic diagram of an air knife (2)

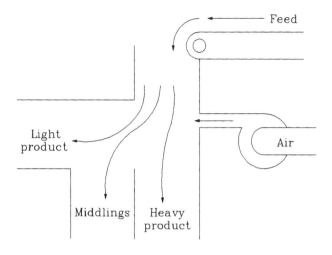

FIGURE 20. Schematic diagram of an air knife (3)

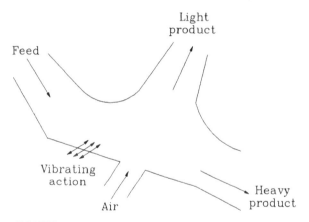

FIGURE 21. Vibrating air classifier

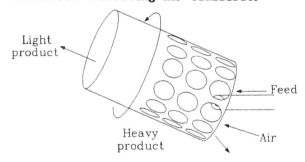

FIGURE 22. Rotary air classifier

A detailed description on the theory of operation, etc., of air classifiers can also be found in *Unit Operations in Resource Recovery Engineering*[38].

2.2.3.2 Rising current separation

Rising current (RC) separation is otherwise known as water elutriation, wet classification, or water current separation (WCS).

The theory behind RC separation is virtually the same as for air classification, except of course that water is used as the elutriating fluid rather than air. Water classification utilizes a rising current of water to carry light particles while dense particles sink. It gives comparable results to heavy media separation of shredder residues using a galena-in-water suspension[6]. An experimental water elutriating column is shown in Figures 23 and 24[48]. The results obtained in this USBM separator, when used on non-magnetic residue gave recoveries as follows:

- 49% copper, 97% zinc, 52% aluminium, 100% lead and 96% iron.

There are several industrial versions of this type of separator, such as the Wemco rising-current separator (Figure 25)[24] and the Newell Industries water current separator (WCS). The WCS consists of a steel tank structure with an internal conveyor. There are two compartments, in one there is a strong upflow of water which separates the non-ferrous metals from the waste. The non-ferrous fraction sinks and is collected on a conveyor under water and taken into the second compartment, and then out on another conveyor. The waste is light enough to be washed over the side onto a dewatering screen. This system can beneficiate non-ferrous metals to 40-60% metal content with normal autoshredder non-magnetic reject[42].

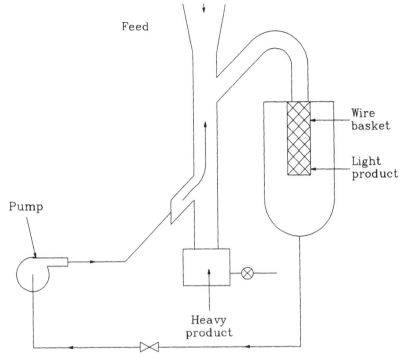

FIGURE 23.   Water elutriating column (1)

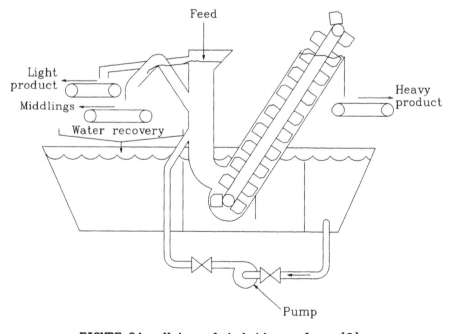

FIGURE 24.   Water elutriating column (2)

2.2.3.3 Gravity concentrators

Gravity methods of separation are used extensively in the minerals processing industries, but unfortunately their application is limited in resource recovery because, apart from the mineral jig, the normal maximum size of feed is about 3 mm[49]. The main potential application for gravity concentration methods is for fine granulator products such as copper/plastic electrical scrap (air tables are used quite widely for this application).

Gravity concentration methods separate minerals of different specific gravity by their relative movement in response to gravity and one or more other forces, the latter often being the resistance to motion offered by a viscous fluid, such as water or air. The principles of gravity concentration are discussed in *Mineral Processing Technology*[49], and a comprehensive description of the application of a wide range of gravity concentration devices employed in minerals engineering is also given.

Mineral Jigs. The jig is a device that achieves the separation of light and heavy particles by using their different abilities to penetrate an oscillating bed. The bed is rendered fluid by a pulsating current of water to produce stratification. The aim is to dilate the bed of material being treated and to control the dilation so that the heavier, smaller particles penetrate the interstices of the bed and the larger high specific gravity particles fall under a condition of hindered settling. The pulsating current of water is set up by, for instance, a plunger in the water. A screen is used to support the bed, heavy particles are removed through a port in the side, while light particles are washed over a weir at the top of the jig (Figure 26)[38,49]. USBM used jigging and tabling on the minus ¼" fraction of non-magnetic autoshredder rejects - the jig proved to be the most promising but unfortunately satisfactory results could not be obtained[43].

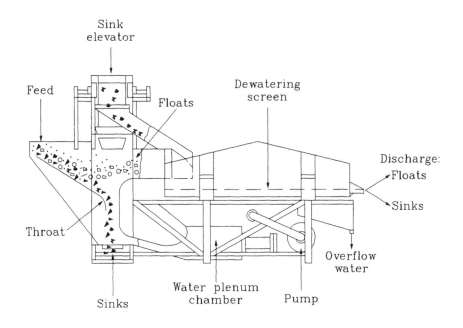

FIGURE 25. Rising-current separator

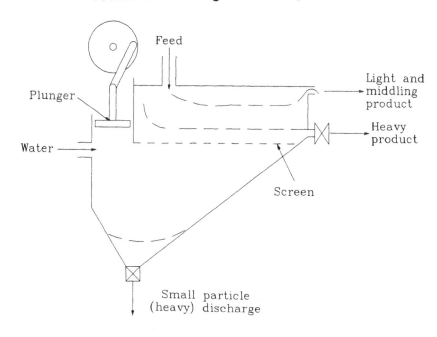

FIGURE 26. Plunger-type mineral jig

Pneumatic tables. Also known as air tables or stoners. These were originally developed for seed separation, and this development has been continued by the minerals industries. Pneumatic tables use a throwing motion to move the feed along a flat riffled deck, and blow air continuously up through a porous bed. The stratification produced means that both the particle size and the density decrease from the top of the concentrate band to the tailings, the coarse particles in the middlings band having the lowest density. Air tables have been applied for the recovery of aluminium from shredded and screened waste, and for the separation of copper from plastic insulated wire scrap. They are most frequently employed where the two-part separation into light and heavy fractions involves a minor fraction of heavies, with a density difference between the two of at least 1.5 : 1[38,49].

Shaking tables. These are the most metallurgically efficient form of gravity concentrator but their application to salvage operations appears to be limited (Figure 27). They consist of a slightly inclined deck A onto which feed (at about 25% solids by weight) is introduced at the feed box and is distributed along C; wash water is distributed along the balance of the feed side from launder D. The table is vibrated longitudinally, by the mechanism B, using a slow forward stroke and a rapid return, which causes the mineral particles to "crawl" along the deck parallel to the direction of motion. The minerals are thus subjected to two forces - one due to the table motion and a second, perpendicular to it, due to the flowing film of water. The net effect is that the particles move diagonally across the deck from the feed end and, since the effect of the film depends on the size and density of the particles, they will fan out on the table, the smaller, denser particles riding highest towards the concentrate launder at the far end, while the larger lighter particles are washed into the tailings launder, which runs along the length of the table[38,49].

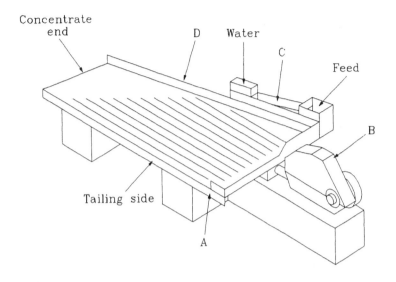

FIGURE 27. Wet shaking table

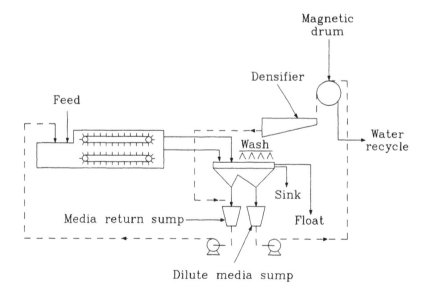

FIGURE 28. Heavy medium separation plant

2.2.3.4 Heavy media separation

Also known as sink-float separation, dense media separation (DMS) and HMS. Very dense media may be used to support the majority of the materials in a waste stream, allowing only selected high density materials to sink and pass out of the separation device at the bottom of the media container. The basis of HMS is the creation of a fluid of specific gravity such that materials in a given specific gravity range either float to the surface and are recovered, or sink to the bottom of the vessel and are removed from there (Figure 28)[12,24].

Dense liquids such as bromoform (sp.gr. 2.89) can be used as the separating fluid, but these tend to be hazardous to health as they are usually long chain hydrocarbons, which produce dangerous fumes and injure the skin on contact. It is also difficult to vary the density of these liquids so suspensions of finely divided solid particles in water have been developed. Suitable solids are magnetite and ferrosilicon, which not only have high specific gravities but they can also be recovered by magnetic separation[12]. *Wemco cone separator.* This type of heavy medium separator is widely used for ore treatment, since it has a relatively high sinks capacity, and should therefore be applicable to autoshredder residues. The cone can have a diameter of up to 6 m and can accommodate feed particles of up to 100 mm in diameter, with capacities of up to 500 tons per hour. The feed is introduced onto the surface of the medium by free-fall, which allows it to plunge several centimetres into the medium. Gentle agitation by rakes mounted onto the central shaft helps keep the medium in suspension. The float fraction simply overflows a weir, whilst the sinks are removed by pump or by internal or external airlift[49]. A dense medium separation plant will always contain a medium recovery section as an integral part of the process. The recovery section consists of washing screens, medium recovery, medium reconsitution and reuse components.

Drum separators. These are built in several sizes, up to 4.3 m diameter by 6 m long, with maximum capacities of 450 tons per hour, and can treat feeds of up to 300 mm in diameter. Separation is achieved by the continuous removal of the sink product through the action of lifters fixed to the inside of the rotating drum (Figure 29). The lifters empty into the sink launder when they pass the horizontal position. The float product overflows a weir at the opposite end of the drum from the feed chute. Longitudinal partitions separate the float surface from the sink-discharge action of the revolving lifters. The comparatively shallow pool depth means that there is minimal settling out of the medium particles, giving a uniform gravity throughout the drum[49].

Two-compartment drum separator. Where single stage HMS is unable to achieve the desired recovery, two-stage separation can be employed. This is, in effect, two drum separators mounted integrally and rotating together, one feeding the other. The lighter medium in the first compartment separates a pure float product. The sink is lifted and conveyed into the second compartment where the middlings and the true sinks are separated[49].

Centrifugal separators. Cyclone heavy media separators are widely used in the treatment of ores and coal. They provide a high centrifugal force and a low viscosity in the medium, enabling much finer separations to be achieved than in gravitational heavy media separators. Various types have been developed, some based directly on the hydrocyclone (the only difference being the density of the carrying fluid, i.e. not water), and others of new design, such as the *Tri-Flo* and *Dyna Whirlpool* separators.

Magnetic fluid separators. If a magnetic fluid is subjected to high magnetic fields, the levitation force of the magnetic fluid can create densities of up to 10 g cm^{-3}, and separators can be constructed utilizing this effect (Figures 30, 31, 32)[53,54].

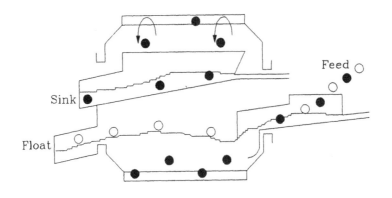

FIGURE 29.   Dense medium drum separator

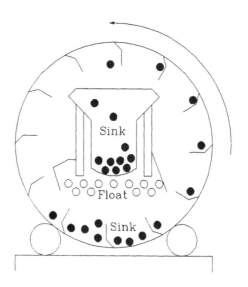

FIGURE 29a.   Drum separator (end view)

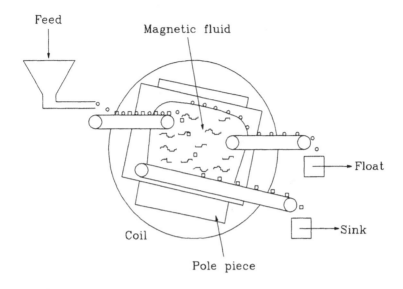

FIGURE 30. Magnetic fluid separator (1)

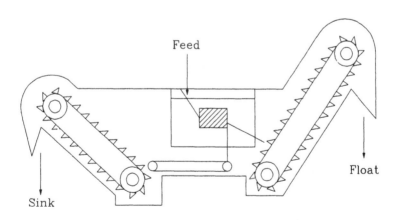

FIGURE 31. Magnetic fluid separator (2)

The use of magnetic fluids may be attractive for large-scale operations to separate the denser materials found in MSW. The distinct advantage of a magnetic fluid is that many more particles with a broader range of densities can be removed (Figure 33). The figure illustrates the density of various non-ferrous metals and the range of those metals which HMS and magnetic fluids will separate. For example, HMS will only effectively separate aluminium from other materials. The proper application of magnetic fluids may permit the separation of such diverse items as platinum and aluminium[38].

Figure 34 illustrates a typical prototype magnetic fluid separation process. In the operation, incoming shredded mixed metals are placed in a static pool of magnetic fluid suspended between the poles of an electromagnet. Depending on the apparent density of the material being separated, the material must either float to the top of the pool or sink to the bottom. Floating and sinking particles are conveyed to separate locations for further washing and removal of the magnetic fluid. In this operation, mixtures of three or more components, such as aluminium, copper and lead may be separated in a multipass operation. The aluminium would be separated in the first pass, then the copper and lead in the second by changing the apparent density of the magnetic fluid by increasing the magnetic field strength[38].

2.2.3.5 Ballistic/inertial separators

The density or specific gravity of a material provides a direct measure of the force necessary to produce a given acceleration in a given volume of material. This measure of force per unit volume necessary for a given acceleration is termed inertia. Thus differences in material density cause differences in the inertial properties of different materials. So, if a group of particles of identified size but varying composition are all propelled by a given force, the material with the greatest amount of inertia will

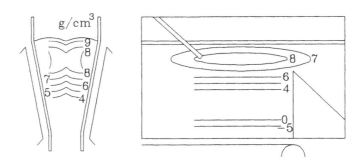

FIGURE 32.   Distribution of the levitation force in a magnetic fluid separation cell

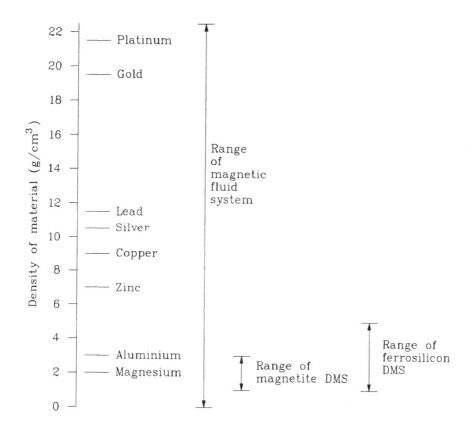

FIGURE 33.   Separation ranges of DMS and magnetic fluid separation systems

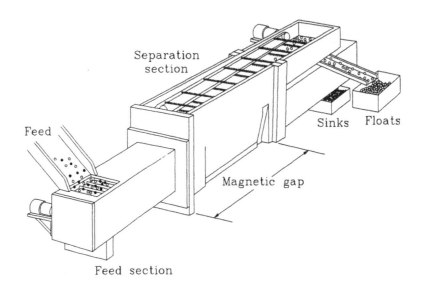

FIGURE 34.   Magnetic fluid separation, adapted from Reference 38

travel the shortest distance. If the same group of particles have the same acceleration applied to them, then the material with the greatest inertia will travel the furthest distance[12].

The inertial properties of materials have been used in conjunction with air resistance of particles in proposed separation systems which have been given the name *ballistic separators,* where the winnowing action of an air stream may be used to improve the efficiency of separation (Figures 35, 36, 37, 38)[6,12,24].

Inertial separators have been developed which combine inertial properties of the material with other properties such as resilience. With the exception of the horizontal rotor hammermill which acts as a ballistic separator in rejecting heavy metallic particles, no successful application of inertial separators has been made for solid wastes. The masking effects of the various constituents in solid wastes have prevented the effective separation of materials[12].

2.2.3.6 Fluidised bed separators

Another method of achieving density separation is to use a *pneumatically fluidised bed.* The medium consists of a solid, such as sand, iron powder or magnetite set into fluid-like action by the passage of low pressure air through an inclined porous base. Care must be taken to establish conditions which achieve the correct density but, this being done, the fluidized particles will exhibit many of the properties of a true fluid. The range of effective densities is from less than 1 gcm^{-3} to more than 4 gcm^{-3}. An example of a practical use is the separation of aluminium and copper from shredded car radiators[3,6].

Another example is the *fluidized bed separator* developed by Warren Spring Laboratory (WSL - Figure 39). It was developed to remove the non-ferrous fraction of incinerator residues but is also applicable to physically separated waste streams.

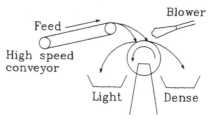

FIGURE 35.   Ballistic separator (1)

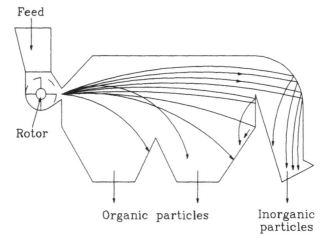

FIGURE 36.   Ballistic separator (2)

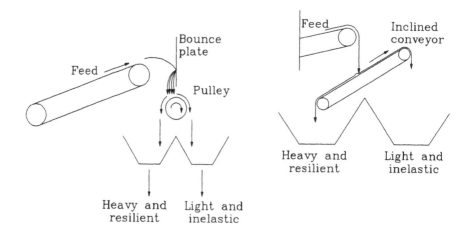

FIGURES 37 & 38.   Inclined conveyor-type separators

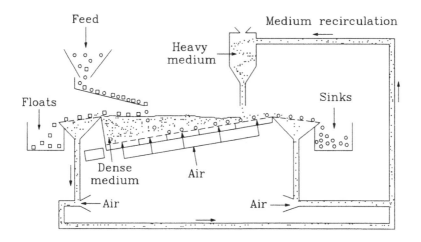

FIGURE 39. Fluidised bed separator

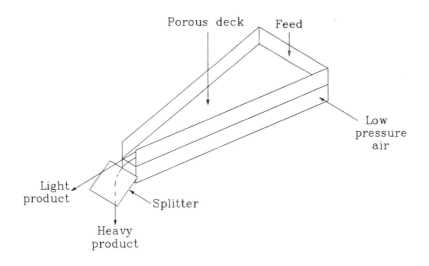

FIGURE 40. Pneumatic pinched sluice separator

Preliminary tests showed favourable results at comparatively low operating costs - on average the non-ferrous fraction of incinerator residue contains 45% aluminium, 25% copper and smaller amounts of lead, zinc and nickel. The WSL separator succeeded in upgrading these into an aluminium rich (95%) and a copper rich (60%) fraction. The medium used was ferrosilicon which was screened out from the products (operates on plus 1.7 mm feeds)[3,31].

For finer particles, WSL developed a *pneumatic pinched sluice* which uses direct air fluidization (Figure 40). The mixture to be separated is fed into the wider end of a sloping porous deck, through which low pressure air is blown. During the fluidized flow the heavier particles sink and move at lower velocity because of frictional contact with the deck surface. The lighter layers move more rapidly and follow a different discharge path at the lower end where they are separated by a product splitter into light and heavy fractions. Both the pneumatic pinched sluice and the fluidized bed separator have been used successfully to separate plastic and metal from granulated insulated wire scrap[6,31].

2.2.4 SEPARATION BY DIFFERENCES IN MAGNETIC PROPERTIES

Differences in the ferromagnetic properties of materials can be used to effect a separation. Coding occurs when the ferromagnetic material interacts with a magnetic field, and separation is caused by magnetic attraction, while the non-ferrous materials (non-magnetic stainless steels are regarded here as non-ferrous) are separated by gravity prior to release of the magnetic field. The use of the force associated with a magnetic field gradient for the extraction of ferrous materials is probably one of the simplest, most effective and economical processes used to separate components of MSW. It is a well known technique, used first for the removal of tramp iron and for the concentration of ores[38].

There are two general categories of use: for the purification of feed streams containing unwanted magnetic impurities, and for the concentration of magnetic materials. Conventional *magnetic separation devices* applied to the salvage industry are generally restricted to separating ferromagnetic materials, such as iron and magnetite. High intensity separators, which have been developed for the minerals processing industries, are able to separate feebly paramagnetic materials, but because of size constraints these are not generally applicable to resource recovery except for the separation of different coloured glass, which is coloured by its iron content, and with the use of large particle high intensity magnetic separators such as DICUS, below[6,38].

Magnetic separators are usually situated directly after the primary shredder, or just after the air classifier (if used). Occasionally secondary magnetic separators are utilized to retrieve the 10 - 20% of ferrous metal missed by the primary separator. It is often necessary to reshred and then air classify a magnetic concentrate to free contaminants such as the contents of tin cans[38,39].

There are two types of magnetic separator which have found acceptance in salvage operations. The first is the holding type separator, where waste is fed directly onto the collecting surface, and the second is the suspended type, where the collecting surface must pick up ferrous material from among non-magnetic particles. Both of these are dry separators, wet separators tend to be used only for the recovery of medium from HMS operations (Figure 41). The design parameters include field intensity and field gradient systems, the mechanical means by which waste is brought to the magnet, the type of magnet (permanent or electro), whether the magnet is stationary or moving, and the height of the magnet over the feed belt[38]. Detailed discussion can be found in *Mineral Processing Technology*[49].

Drum wash

■ Magnetics

o Non-magnetics

FIGURE 41.   Wet drum low intensity magnetic separator

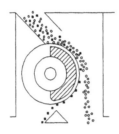

FIGURE 42.   Dry drum low intensity magnetic separator

FIGURE 43.   Alternating pole arrangement inside drum

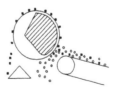

FIGURE 44.   Dry drum low intensity magnetic separator

Drum separators. These separators are of the holding type and consist of a rotating horizontal cylinder made of a non-magnetic material such as brass or stainless steel (Figure 42). The drum surrounds a magnetic bank which is formed in the same shape as the drum itself. As material flows onto the drum the magnetic material is collected and carried to a point below a doctoring blade or brush, out of the influence of the magnetic field, and is scraped off the drum. The non-magnetic materials drop directly off the drum under gravity. The quality of the material removed by drum separators is generally quite poor, but it can be improved by having alternating poles inside the drum which agitate the material to shake off non-magnetic debris (Figure 43). Drums can have a diameter between 30 to 75 cm and a width up to 1.5 m[19,24,38,55]. Another configuration of drum type separator, where only the magnetics come into contact with the collecting surface is shown in Figure 44[39].

Belt/magnetic pulley separators. These are another form of holding type separators. Belt separators have a fixed magnetic assembly inside an end pulley (Figure 45) and magnetic pulley separators have a rotating magnetic pulley at the end of a conveyor belt (Figure 46). A thin layer of feed is fed directly onto the collecting surface by the conveyor belt and the rest of the separation process is similar to that of a drum separator. The pulley diameter can be between 30 to 60 cm and the belt up to 2.5 m in width. Magnetic pulleys tend not to be widely used on MSW[19,24,38]. There are some resource recovery applications for this type of separator, however. One is the separation of mixed used beverage cans (UBCs), where aluminium cans are separated from steel cans, and another, developed by British Steel Corporation is used as a scrap density sorter (Figure 47)[56,57,58]. Here mixed light and heavy steel scrap are separated - the heavy scrap is removed under gravity, but the light scrap is light enough to be attracted to the belt by the weak magnetic field.

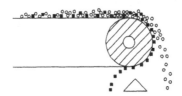

FIGURE 45.   Belt-type holding separator

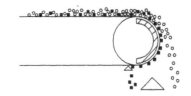

FIGURE 46.   Magnetic pulley

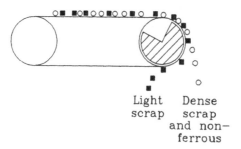

FIGURE 47.   Scrap density magnetic separator

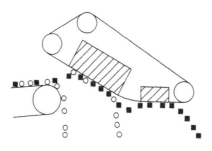

FIGURE 48.   Suspended belt magnetic separator

Overband magnetic separators.   Overband/suspended belt type magnetic separators are preferred for use on MSW (Figure 48). None of the feed comes into direct contact with the collecting surface, as in the holding type separator.   Feed is conveyed through a relatively strong magnetic field gradient which lifts ferrous material from surrounding medium and attaches it to the belt by the strength of the magnetic field and the magnitude of the field gradient.   In order to shake off entrained particles there may be a break in the magnetic field to let the ferrous drop off under gravity and then be picked up by the next magnet along. Overband magnetic separators may be situated in-line or across the conveyor belt carrying the feed[19,38].

DICUS large particle high intensity magnetic separator.   DICUS (DIrect CUrrent Separator) was developed by Vanderbilt University and Magnetic Separation Systems, Inc., of Nashville, Tennessee. It is a high intensity, high gradient magnetic separator, capable of handling large feed sizes (up to 15 cm) and is, thus, unlike other high intensity magnetic separators, applicable to scrap feeds and includes in its list of materials separated:

- Austenitic and ferritic stainless steels
- Manganese steel
- Tungsten carbide
- Automobile scrap (chrome plated materials)
- Superalloys such as Hastelloy, Inconel and K-monel

The separator is similar to a magnetic pulley type low intensity separator in construction except that it has an external, water-cooled electro-magnet which surrounds the magnetic pulley and focuses a high gradient magnetic field over the open faced separating surface of the active region.   This technology does not appear to have been widely researched or reported - with the introduction of superconducting magnets and high energy permanent magnets it could offer a low running cost method for concentrating the non-ferrous fraction of autoshredder residues.

2.2.5 SEPARATION BY DIFFERENCES IN ELECTRICAL CONDUCTIVITY

There are three basic types of *conductivity separators*: electrostatic (high tension) separator, eddy current separator and conductivity sorter. They all separate particles on the basis of differences in electrical conductivity, and are therefore particularly suited to the separation of metals from most non-metals.

2.2.5.1 Electrostatic (high-tension) separators

There are two types of action which act on particles in *electrostatic separators*. The "lifting effect" is the attraction of a charged particle in an electric field towards an electrode of opposite polarity. Materials which have a tendency to become charged with a definite polarity may be separated from each other by use of the lifting effect even if their conductivities are very similar - this is pure electrostatic separation, but it suffers from inefficiency and temperature sensitivity.

Most industrial processes make use of the "pinning effect". Non-conducting particles receive a surface charge from the electrode, retain their charge, and are pinned to the opposite charged separator surface (Figure 49) by positive-negative attraction. Both the pinning effect and the holding effect can be used together[6,49,59].

2.2.5.2 Eddy current separators

In an electrical conductor, the induced voltage due to changes in magnetic induction will produce a current known as an eddy current. The direction of the eddy current loop is determined by Lenz's Law: if the magnetic flux density B is increasing, the current direction will be such as to create a magnetic field that opposes the applied magnetic field; if B is decreasing, the current direction will be such as to create a magnetic field that reinforces the applied field[38].

In an aluminium can, for example, if the magnetic field is increasing, an eddy current flows and the can, in effect, becomes a solenoid with its north pole pointing to the north pole of the applied field (or vice-versa). Therefore it will be repelled by the applied field, effecting a coding (recognition of its magnetic polarity) and a separation (by the forces due to magnetic repulsion)[38].

The force that orients a current loop or bar magnet in a stationary magnetic field, and that moves a current loop or bar magnet in a moving magnetic field is called the Lorentz force. If the field is uniform over the can, the net Lorentz force is zero (as it is a vector product). If, however, the field were stronger on one side of the can than on the other, the can would be propelled in the direction in which the magnetic flux density (B) was increasing (the maximum Lorentz force can be expected when B is in one direction on one side of the can and the opposite direction on the other side of the can)[38].

When the magnetic field is moved (as a travelling B sine wave) by electrically phasing the current to the motor windings, any conductors containing eddy currents will experience a net force in the direction of field motion. Similarly, if the conducting materials move through a stationary, but alternating (-N-S-N-S-...) magnetic field, they will experience a Lorentz force in the direction connecting adjacent N-S poles[38].

There are four methods of inducing eddy currents in metals[38]:

● Physically move a sample through a magnetic field
● Move the magnetic field through the sample by moving the magnet
● Move the magnetic field through the sample by an electrical phasing technique
● Temporarily change the magnetic field intensity in a sample

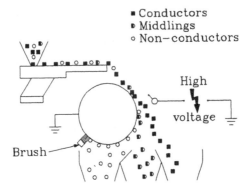

FIGURE 49.   Schematic diagram of an electrostatic drum separator

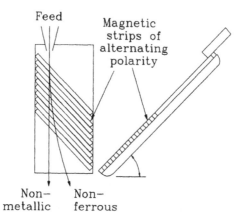

FIGURE 50.   Schematic diagram of an inclined table separator

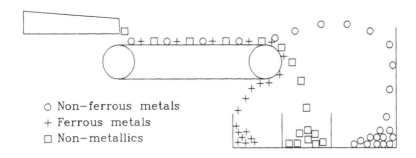

FIGURE 51.   Schematic diagram of an eddy current separator

Such methods could be used, for example, to separate aluminium from glass (this is not possible by a gravity separation process as glass and aluminium have such a small density difference). Since the effect depends on the ability of a magnetic field to levitate the conductor by repulsion, the ratio of conductivity to density provides a measure of discrimination amongst metals.

TABLE 8. Ratio of conductivity to density of various metals[38].

Metal	Electrical conductivity, σ (mho/m)	Mass density, ρ (kg/m^3)	σ/ρ mho - m/kg
Aluminium	0.35×10^8	2.7×10^3	13.0×10^3
Copper	0.59 "	8.9 "	6.7 "
Silver	0.63 "	10.5 "	6.0 "
Zinc	0.17 "	7.1 "	2.4 "
Brass	0.14 "	8.5 "	1.7 "
Tin	0.09 "	7.3 "	1.2 "
Lead	0.05 "	11.3 "	0.4 "

Early in the development of eddy current separators, most effort was involved in the use of *linear induction motors* (LIMs). These were used in several different designs of machine, such as that produced by Cotswold Research Ltd.[60], with LIMs situated above, below, and in tandem around the conveyor belt carrying the feed, and also in vertical separators which work under gravity. These separators, however, can be energy intensive and hence expensive to run[38].

Inclined table separators which use alternating polarity permanent magnetic strips across a table were developed (Figure 50), but these have not been commercially accepted, probably due to feed, efficiency and throughput restrictions[38].

With the development of high energy permanent magnets simple low energy non-ferrous separation systems have been developed.

The alternating magnetic field is created by a high speed cylindrical assembly of permanent magnets (up to 3000 RPM) which rotate inside an outer drum onto/over which the material passes. The materials leave the drum in various product splits – non-ferrous metal which is thrown clear of the drum; non-metallics which leave the drum under gravity; and ferrous metals, which are attracted to the drum until brushed off (Figure 51)[61].

Newell Engineering Ltd. claim a reduction in capital cost of 75% compared to LIMs and a 98% reduction in energy input with greatly improved separation efficiency for their Non-Ferrous Separator, which is a permanent magnet eddy current separator with a capacity of approximately 5-4 t/hr (Figure 52)[62].

2.2.5.3 Conductivity sorters

A third method of separation by the use of differences in electrical conductivity is the use of a *conductivity sorter*. One or more of a series of electrical probes maintained at a steady potential with respect to an earthing conductor makes contact with each item and the current flow through the article codes it on the basis of conductivity, or a conductivity coil codes it on the basis of induced eddy current through the coil, and this permits the article to be diverted by an air blast or similar sorting device (Figure 53)[6]. This type of separation device is a form of ore sorter (see below).

2.2.6 SEPARATION BY ELECTRONIC SORTING METHODS

Hand sorting is the original form of ore sorting technique. *Electronic ore sorting*, where individual particles are removed from the feed stream, after coding by one or more properties, by a device such as an air blast switch was first produced in the late 1940s for use on mineral feedstocks[49].

Sorting is feasible when the raw feed constituents are suitably liberated at a size usually greater than 10 mm. Sorters

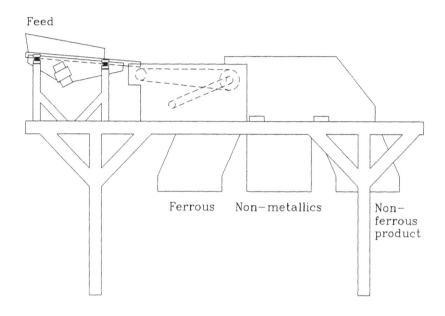

FIGURE 52. The Newell Engineering eddy current separator

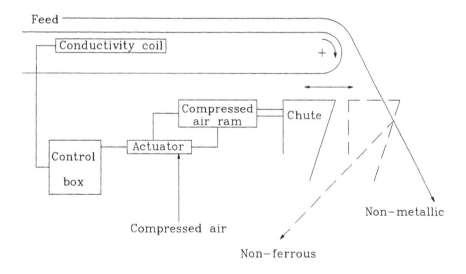

FIGURE 53. Schematic diagram of a conductivity sorter

assess the difference in a specific physical property between the particles and send a control signal to a mechanical or electrical device which removes valuable particles from the stream (Figure 54)[55]. It is therefore essential that a distinct difference in the required physical property is apparent between the values and the waste. Particles should be thoroughly washed before sorting to avoid blurring of the signal and the feed should undergo preliminary screening[49].

Electromagnetic radiation (from microwave through infra-red, visual, ultra-violet and X-rays to gamma radiation) is the most widely used coding utilized in electronic sorting. The optical scanner, using visible radiation, can separate optically transparent from opaque materials, for example glass from aluminium) and as a colour sorter can separate on a colour basis, for example flint from green from amber glass. The spectrum of infra-red radiation diffusely reflected from a surface shows all the major infra-red absorption lines characteristic of the reflector and this information can be electronically processed in order to separate materials[6].

2.2.6.1 Photometric sorters

Photometric (or colour or optical) sorting has been used for a long time in the mineral processing industries, especially for the colour sorting of diamonds, and in the food and agricultural industries, for example the sorting of kernels of corn on the basis of reflective properties. There is, therefore, potential for optical sorting of solid waste[12].

Photometric sorting is a mechanized form of hand sorting, in which the materials are separated into components of different value by visual examination. The basis of the photometric sorter is a laser light source and a sensitive photomultiplier, using a scanning system to detect light reflected from the surfaces of particles passing through the sorting zone. Electronic circuitry analyses the photomultiplier signal which changes with the intensity of the reflected light and produces control signals to actuate the appropriate valves of an air blast rejection device to remove certain particles selected by means of the analysing procedure[49].

A typical machine is the *Gunson's Sortex MP60* machine which can handle materials in the 10 - 150 mm size range at feed rates of up to 150 t h^{-1}. A monolayer of randomly spaced particles moving at the same velocity is set up and these particles are thrown through a quartz-halogen lit viewing zone. Here a solid-state camera scans the individual particles at one thousand times a second using an array of 1024 photosensors. This builds up a virtually complete spectral picture of the exposed surface, and provides information as to the speed and flight path of the particle. With this information a microprocessor decides whether to accept or reject the particle, and which air blast switch to use[49].

An earlier design is the *Sortex G414 Colour Separator* (Figure 55) which uses photocells to compare particles against coloured backgrounds. The signal is amplified and discoloured items are removed from the main stream by an air jet[55].

The *RTZ Ore Sorters Model 16* is another make of photometric sorter (Figure 56). High intensity laser light is reflected off a rotating mirror drum and is able to scan at 2000 times per second[49].

2.2.6.2 X-ray sorting

In the mineral industry, *X-ray sorting* is used to concentrate diamonds, which fluoresce under a beam of X-rays. This fluorescence can be detected by photomultipliers[49].

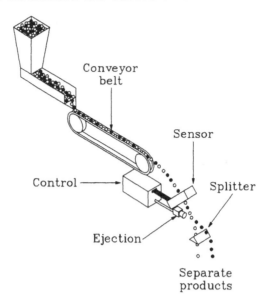

FIGURE 54.   Schematic diagram of an electronic sorter

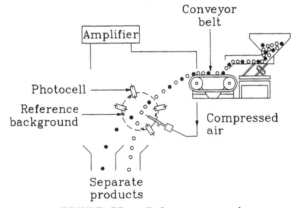

FIGURE 55.   Colour separator

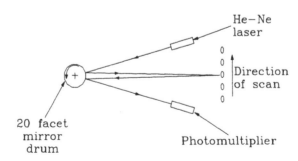

FIGURE 56.   Photometric sorter

2.2.6.3 Gamma ray sorting

Although not applicable to resource recovery, uranium emits gamma rays which can be detected by a commercial NaI (Th) scintillation detector, and can hence be sorted. Another form of *gamma sorting* is used to beneficiate beryllium ores - the mineral is exposed to gamma radiation and a photoneutron is released which can be detected[49].

2.2.6.4 Neutron absorption sorting

Another method not necessarily applicable to resource recovery, *neutron absorption separation* is used in the sorting of boron minerals. The ore is exposed to a neutron source and the neutron flux attenuation is detected and used as the means of sorting[49].

2.2.6.5 Conductivity/magnetic response sorter

Based on the conductivity sorter (see above), the *RTZ Ore Sorters Model 19* conductivity/magnetic response sorter remotely measures the electrical conductivity and magnetic susceptibility of individual particles. The detectors respond to only slight variations in such properties, and are suitable for use on a wide variety of ores such as native metals and, presumably, also on scrap metal. At its upper size range of 150 mm the feed rate can be as high as 120 t h^{-1}. Once the main detectors have assessed the particle, it is optically examined for its size and shape and the system then calculates the grade from the size and magnetic/conductivity response[49].

2.2.6.6 Gamma scattering sorting

Precon developed by Outokumpu of Finland is a preconcentrating device which can be used on feeds where there is at least a 5% metal difference between valuable and waste particles. The most suitable metals are chromium, iron, cobalt, nickel, copper and zinc, or any combination of these. The system uses a gamma scattering analysis and can handle up to 15 particles per second. For 150 mm lumps the feed rate can be as high as 40 t h^{-1} (Figures 57 and 58)[49,63].

2.2.6.7 Others

Sequential heating and infra-red scanning has been used to sort asbestos[49].

Scheelite has been sorted using the fact that it fluoresces under ultra-violet radiation[49].

High powered pulsed lasers or spark beams can be used to vapourise a very small portion of an object and the resulting vapour can be analysed in a manner similar to flame photometry - precise classification of materials is possible in theory[6].

It may be possible in the future to sort using the technology utilized in the Outokumpu high speed X-ray fluorescence (XRF) metal alloy identifier[64].

2.2.7 OTHER METHODS OF PHYSICAL CONCENTRATION

2.2.7.1 Bounce and slide methods

Hard materials can be separated from soft materials by dropping them on to a moving belt - the hard bounce off and the soft remain, for example glass from compost. A much more precise use of resilience is the impact sensor, used as an ore sorter. Items are struck by a tool on which an accelerometer is mounted and the deceleration of the tool depends on the material[6].

The difference in frictional resistance between various materials can be used as a basis for separation. If a mixture is launched at a striker/slider plate then the materials with the highest frictional resistance will have a shorter trajectory than those with the least resistance[6].

2.2.7.2 Length separator

Length separators are a form of size separator (Figure 59)[58] but

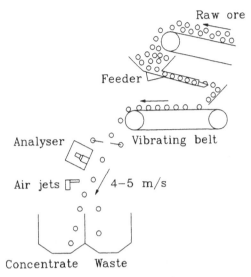

FIGURE 57.   Schematic of the Precon sorting system

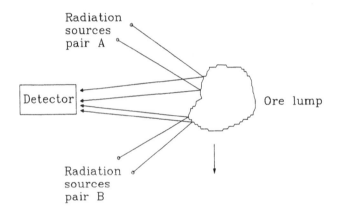

FIGURE 58.   Gamma-scattering principle of operation

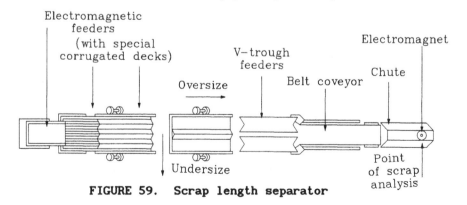

FIGURE 59.   Scrap length separator

have been dealt with separately here as they separate on the basis of one dimension (i.e. length) as opposed to separation by two dimensions used in screening.   A vibratory bed aligns the different scrap which is passed over ever-increasing gaps which sequentially sort the short from the long pieces of scrap.

2.2.7.3 Vibratory sorters

Commonly used in the scrap metal industry, vibratory sorters consist of an inclined vibrating deck which if fed to the middle - rubber materials tend to rise up the deck, i.e. against gravity, while metallics move down the deck, hence a separation is achieved which has relied on the differences between the coefficient of friction for the material/deck contact for different materials.

2.3 SUMMARY

Physical separation methods can produce alloy concentrates suitable for recycling from such diverse sources as autoshredders, MSW processing plants and incinerators.   Experienced scrap sorters, using object recognition, spark tests, chemical spot tests, colour, apparent density and magnetic properties can adequately sort a wide variety of alloy groups[65].

The complex nature of new materials entering the scrap market has made sorting more difficult and expensive.   Many alloys contain so many components that separation as discreet alloys becomes a prerequisite for efficient recycling.   The amount of sorting done is dependant on the premium paid for better segregated materials and the premium tends to increase as the inherent value of scrap increases.   For example, segregated superalloys have a value of $1 per pound more than mixed superalloy scrap[65].

Current research aims to improve recycling by the introduction of new technology to identify and sort metals, such as[65]:

Aluminium alloys - hardness and eddy current used to segregate alloys

Superalloys - thermoelectric response, emission spectography, XRF spectography, and spark testing that can be done by machine rather than man.

CHAPTER THREE

THE PROCESSING OF FRAGMENTIZED METAL WASTES

The motor vehicle is complex and self-contaminating, characteristics which make reclamation difficult, but processing for efficient recycling is highly desirable as scrap vehicles represent the most important single resource of re-usable metals, plastics and rubber in developed countries[43,69].

Most automobiles have a lifetime of between 8 to 12 years and domestic appliances such as refrigerators, washing machines, etc., have a lifetime of approximately 12 to 13 years[66,67,68]. Once this period has elapsed and the unit is ready to be discarded the value to the owner has declined to near zero and interest in the product has changed from one of utility to one of disposal. The route of easiest disposal is usually sought rather than the most cost effective, this leads to units being randomly dumped and, in the case of domestic appliances, means a lack of a centrally-located continuous source of supply for a processor. Consequently, domestic appliances have to be processed along with another source of scrap metal. This is usually the motor car because the other main source of discarded steel consumer products is urban waste (containers), and the similarities between systems for handling automobiles and domestic appliances are greater than those between containers and domestic appliances[68].

In 1976 there were 109 million automobiles and 35 million commercial vehicles in the United States[69]. By 1990 this number had risen to approximately 180 million automobiles, a third of the world's total of 550 million automobiles[1]. Forty million cars a year were being produced in 1979, and this number increased by a third in the following decade[1,70].   In the mid-seventies only 8 million cars per year were being processed for scrap in the United States despite a total inventory of 12 million junk cars in 1973, by 1990 the number of cars being processed had risen to 10 million[1,6,27,67].   In the United Kingdom approximately a million autos per year are processed, with another million being held or in storage, and the world total for 1990 was approximately 30 million[1,24,71].   In 1980 approximately 29 million domestic appliance units were available for processing in the United States[68].

The steel reclaimed from old scrap such as automobiles and white goods represents a significant part of the steel reclamation cycle.   In developed countries, discarded road vehicles form the major source of post-consumer ferrous scrap, whose availability is significantly affected by price.   This cannot be offset by high prices for non-ferrous metals as the primary incentive for recycling of scrap cars is the recovery of iron and steel (approximately 80% by weight).   The same applies to domestic appliances, up to 2.6 million tonnes per annum of ferrous metals could be recovered from domestic appliances in the United States alone[16,24,68,71].

In 1990 the potential recovery of steel from automobiles was about 25 million tonnes, expected to be about 30 million tonnes by 2000, and the potential recovery of aluminium was about 750 000 tonnes, expected to be about 2 million tonnes by 2000. Approximately 40 fragmentizer operators existed in the United Kingdom in 1983, with a capacity of 1 million tonnes, and a similar amount of processing was done in West Germany at the same time[1,46,73].

In addition to the ferrous metals, spares and metals such as lead, copper, zinc and aluminium can be recycled - at present the amount of aluminium used in automobiles is increasing and as it does so aluminium becomes more and more important to the scrap processor. In 1974 approximately 4500 tonnes each of aluminium, copper, zinc and brass were being recycled in the United Kingdom, as processing technology advances so the amounts of these metals being recycled increases[1,16,24,71].

Along with the metals in automobiles there is non-metallic detritus arising from seats, carpets, tyres and other components which has little value, and will continue to do so until uses are found for these non-metallics. There is potential for the combustible fraction to be used for heat generation, but this is not common practice[16,73].

3.1 THE SCRAP INDUSTRY

For many years certain parts of the scrap trade have specialised in the sale of used components from scrapped cars, as shown in Table 9. There has always been a demand for these parts from small garages and individuals, especially where new parts are not available, however dismantling for parts has lost some of its importance as the increased complexity of cars and better warranties has led to fewer home repairs.

The discarded vehicle may go to an auto wrecker, a dismantler who removes the valuable parts for sale, and then onto a scrap merchant for breaking and sorting into ferrous and non-ferrous metals and waste. Alternatively the vehicle may go straight to the large scrap merchant. The most valuable scrap metal units which have not been removed for re-use are removed by hand, such as the battery (lead), the radiator (red brass/gunmetal) and easily removable electric motors. Electrical units are removed when their scrap value is greater than the cost of removal (80% of radiators are removed, compared with only 50% of electrical units). Hulks used to be stripped of their valuable components as approximately 50% of the non-ferrous metals could be removed easily, and were then compressed into a cuboid bale (UK No. 5 bale equivalent to US No. 2 bundle), or they were compressed into a

TABLE 9.   Percentage of re-usable components in motor vehicles[16].

Component	Percentage of re-usable components
Engine	25
Axles, differentials and gears	25
Battery	20
Heater	10
Starter motor, generator	20

scrap log and then sheared.   These methods were not ideal, so shredding was rapidly accepted when it was introduced in the early 1960s   (shredding   was   introduced   to   the   UK   in 1968)[6,16,24,43,74,77].

In developed countries almost all cars and light vans are shredded.   For safety or environmental reasons items such as fuel tanks and storage batteries are removed before the fragmentizer process.   The remaining hulk, usually less than 500 kg, is destroyed into fist-sized chunks by a hammermill or other shredder.   The discharge is magnetically separated and a small amount of non-ferrous metals are normally hand picked.   After this preliminary sorting, the non-magnetics are usually passed to a more specialized scrap merchant[1,16,24,75].

Shredders have a very high capital cost, but high capacity plants have comparatively low operating costs.   They need to have a very large, constant supply of automobiles near to hand.   Mobile car flatteners were developed so that up to 15 automobiles could be carried at one time on a single flat-bed trailer, thus cutting the cost of bringing scrap feed to the shredder[6,69,75].

3.1.1 SCRAP QUALITY

The ferrous part of a scrap car used to be compressed into bales of low grade scrap for subsequent melting. Now the most significant technique for processing scrap is the fragmentizer which can reduce a car into fist-sized chunks in 30 to 60 seconds. Shredded scrap has financial and techno-economic advantages over bales, for instance it is much smaller in size and easier to inspect for non-ferrous contamination. The size range is acceptable to cupolas as well as steelmaking furnaces. Once the auto hulk has been comminuted, a degree of magnetic separation is possible, this leads to a high ferrous content scrap, more constant and a higher grade than traditional, and a non-magnetic portion (more easily sorted non-ferrous fraction)[16,24].

Pre-reduced iron ore pellets can be charged continuously to an electric arc furnace, which gives an advantage over scrap, even though it is more expensive. However, properly prepared automobile and large appliance scrap, as well as tin cans, can also be charged continuously to electric arc furnaces and a mixture of scrap and pellets is a suitable charge. The high surface area/volume ratio facilitates heat transfer and ensures rapid melting in comparison to bales. The physical form of shredded scrap greatly simplifies handling procedures[16,27].

The values of scrap steel depends on purity since the presence of other metals such as copper, zinc and aluminium tend to degrade the quality of the steel obtained. For example the presence of copper in steel adversely affects ductility and the presence of copper on the surface of steel causes edge cracks during hot rolling. It is therefore highly desirable to separate the different metals as thoroughly as possible prior to melting. Variability and unpredictability of tramps reduce the value of the scrap and limit its market. The level of impurities is highly dependant on the degree of separation carried out by the merchant and the scrapyard. At worst bales used to contain whole cars,

including battery, wiring and aluminium cylinder heads - one
survey showed the average content of bales to be: ferrous 84%
(range 64-90%) and copper 0.48% (range 0-2.4%)[6,16,24,27,72].

Apart from copper, No. 5 bales also contain impurities such
as zinc and aluminium, and smaller amounts of nickel, chromium and
lead. The amounts of these impurities are much less for shredded
scrap (copper content 0.2-0.22%). Perhaps of greater importance
is the fact that the standard deviation is much lower being 0.04%
for fragmentized scrap compared with 0.44% for bales, which leads
to the scrap being used with a greater degree of confidence.
Ideally auto scrap should contain less than 0.1% copper. It would
be desirable for all copper in automobiles to be used only in
easily removable units, or be replaced with aluminium.   If
fragmentized automobile scrap is zinc-free then the furnace dust
is zinc-free and can be recycled, rather than providing another
waste disposal problem[16,74,75].

Recovery of metal values from a motor car is not simple.
Failure to separate the non-ferrous fraction from steel means that
it must be classified as low grade, and can reduce the value from
a total of more than $108/car as separate fractions to $65/car as
a single, dirty grade (1985).   Fragmentized scrap has rapidly
gained acceptance and performs well as a portion of the charge for
production of steel and cast iron. It is sometimes felt, however,
that for a price which approaches that of some No.1 grades this
scrap has unreasonably high levels of chromium, molybdenum and
nickel, which generally originates in alloy steels, stainless
irons and clad or plated steels - all of which report to the
magnetic fraction.   Further improvement of shredded scrap is
difficult, since in order to reduce tramp element levels to the
equivalent of those found in quality cold forming sheet, some of
the shredded scrap must be separated out as alloyed fractions - no
existing technology can effect such a separation under current
economic conditions[16].

3.2 AUTOMOBILE COMPOSITION

It is difficult to accurately characterize the feed to fragmentizers due to the large number of makes and models of cars. It is probably acceptable to regard motor cars as members of one of two groups, either American or European/Japanese - American automobiles tend to be larger and contain much more iron and steel (total weight).   In 1969 the USBM published the first readily available study on the composition of automobiles and, along with later published work, remains the only detailed analysis available (Table 10)[43,75,76].

TABLE 10.   Materials and weight distribution of three composite automobiles[43].

Material	Circa 1960 (US)	Mid-1970s (US)	Early 1980s (Japanese)
Steel (kg)	1148	1264	612
Cast Fe (kg)	232	172	55
Cu (kg)	15	22	11
Zn (kg)	24	20	2.4
Al (kg)	23	37	39
Pb (kg)	0.1	0.4	0.4
Rubber (kg)	66	82	53
Glass (kg)	39	43	30
Plastic (kg)	12	59	50
Misc. (kg)	39	59	24
Total (kg)	1599	1757	878
Steel (wt%	70.8	71.8	69.8
Cast Fe (wt%)	14.5	9.8	6.3
Cu (wt%)	0.9	1.3	1.3
Zn (wt%)	1.5	1.1	0.3
Al (wt%)	1.4	2.1	4.4
Pb (wt%)	<.1	<.1	<.1
Rubber (wt%)	4.1	4.7	6
Glass (wt%)	2.5	2.4	4.4
Plastic (wt%)	0.7	3.4	5.7
Misc. (wt%)	2.5	3.4	2.7

The composition of motor cars varies widely with type and make of car and country of origin. Several references quote various compositions, but the most up-to-date available (1990-US) quotes for scrapped automobiles; slightly less than 1 tonne per vehicle of iron and steel; about 30 kg of aluminium; "substantial" amounts of copper lead and zinc (total about 25 kg); about 150 kg (total) of plastics, glass and rubber. Cars produced in 1990 contain somewhat less iron and steel, much more plastic, about 50 kg aluminium, and less zinc[1,16,43,66,67,71,73,74,75,76].

Since the energy shortage crisis in the mid-1970s, the popularity of smaller, fuel efficient automobiles led to a general downsizing and substitution of lighter weight materials. This led to much increased use of newly developed non-ferrous metal alloys, high strength low alloy (HSLA) steels and plastics in order to reduce automobile weights. As a general rule smaller automobiles contain less ferrous metals but as much or more non-ferrous metals than the larger ones[76].

3.3 SHREDDERS

The shredder, along with its associated equipment, is the only mechanical process used by the scrap processor which is capable of removing some of the non-ferrous impurities. The fragmentizer itself performs essentially the same operation as does the ore crusher in liberating values from gangue. The shredded scrap is amenable to magnetic separation with an improved chance that the ferrous and non-ferrous materials will be present as discrete particles[16,33].

There are over 600 shredders worldwide (64 in the United Kingdom - 1985), with power inputs of 1000-6000 HP each. These are easily capable of handling all the cars scrapped, plus scrapped appliances and commercial/industrial sheet metal goods. Nearly 100% recovery of iron scrap can be obtained, and this is accompanied by an outstanding degree of purity (98%) and bulk density $(1.0-1.5 \text{ t/m}^3)$[1,51,73].

There are four main parts to a shredder plant[74]:

- Fragmentizer and feed device
- Dust extraction plant
- Separation plant
- Conveying plant

Fragmentizers tend to be high power input units (Tables 6, 7, Figures 8, 9), although for high capacity plants the operating costs are comparatively low. Automobiles, minus radiators, tyres, batteries, and fuel tanks are ripped into fist sized chunks, generally minus 100 mm in major dimension, although total size range can be between 20-300 mm, in a hammermill at rates of up to 180 tph (a 5000 HP fragmentizer can shred a large American automobile in 30 seconds).

The charged scrap is crushed by swinging hammers which are suspended at the circumference of a rotor which rotates at around 800 rpm. Size reduction is effected by a combination of impact, tensile and shear stresses. The size and specific bulk weight of the shredded scrap is determined by the size and quantity of grid openings of a basket type bottom grid and/or a top grid plate, according to the shredder system. Steel works generally require shredded scrap with a specific bulk weight of about $1-1.3 \text{ t/m}^3$. With higher specific bulk weight, wear and energy consumption per tonne of shredded scrap raise exponentially to such a degree that production of considerably higher specific bulk weights in a single working cycle of the shredder will generally be uneconomical. Higher scrap densities for special purposes such as cooling scrap can be obtained more economically be screening and recrushing the scrap.

The discharge is then magnetically separated on magnetic drum separators to produce a steel fraction, about 75% by weight, and a non-magnetic fraction, which contains non-ferrous metals, rubber, plastics and other combustibles, dirt, glass and other non-combustibles[1,12,13,16,43,69,74,78].

Large volumes of dust and fluff are generated and collected by air sweep, cyclone and baghouse. Unfortunately shredder fluff is contaminated by a small quantity of hazardous materials and the technical and regulatory problems of disposing of the fluff have not all been solved. This led to shredders in New England being shut down for a while in 1988, and similar action has been taken in Europe although it may be argued that regulators have neglected that the pollution caused by abandoned automobiles and appliances can be a much worse problem than that caused by the fluff. Another environmental problem for shredder operators is the generation of blue fumes from vapourized oil and grease and the danger of explosion. Consequently air cleaning systems have hoods connected directly to the fragmentizer. A 200 HP system is required for dust/fume extraction and air classification of shredder reject for a 2000 HP fragmentizer, and the scrubber plant needs to be protected against explosion. One method of solving this problem is to use semi-wet or wet shredders - the water eliminates the risk of explosion, although wet processing has to be used in the subsequent processing[1,77,78,79].

3.4 NON-MAGNETIC PROCESSING

Table 11 gives the approximate composition of the non-ferrous fraction after shredding and magnetic separation of a car of the following composition: Steel 63%, cast iron 16%, aluminium 1%, copper 1%, zinc 0.5%, lead 0.5%, rubber 8%, glass 3%, plastic 5%, misc. 1%[24].

Tables 12 and 13 give alternative values for the composition of non-magnetic shredder reject. Table 12 gives specific values for a composite mixture made up from three separate samples from different shredder operations analysed by USBM[43]; Table 13 gives the range of possible values for any type of automobile/appliance feed[80].

TABLE 11.   **Non-ferrous fraction after shredding and magnetic separation.**

Material	Composition %
Copper	3.5
Zinc	13.0
Aluminium	4.0
Lead	1.5
Iron	12.0
Stainless steel	present
Rubber and other combustibles	24.0
Glass and other non-combustibles	42.0

TABLE 12.   **Analyses of selected shredder non-magnetic rejects[43].**

Material	Composition %
Copper	3.3
Zinc	13.0
Aluminium	3.8
Lead	1.3
Ferrous (including stainless steel)	11.9
Rubber and other combustibles	24.4
Glass and other non-combustibles	42.3

TABLE 13.   **Range of composition of a typical non-magnetic fraction[80].**

Material	Composition %
Copper	2-10
Zinc	6-15
Aluminium	0-40
Lead	0- 2
Iron	0-16
Stainless steel	0- 0.2
Rubber and other combustibles	20-30
Glass and other non-combustibles	30-50

There are a wide range of processes applicable to the processing of the non-magnetic reject of auto shredders. Most begin with a preliminary air separation of the very light, fibrous materials which would absorb water in later wet processing operations, although this type of separation may precede the magnetic separation (in theory this process route leads to a cleaner magnetic fraction as dirt and impurities are partially removed from the iron, but it requires higher capital and operating costs as the windsifter has to treat a much greater amount of material). After magnetic separation approximately one quarter of the fragmentizer output remains, and this fraction contains the majority of the non-ferrous metals[80].

Shredder plants produce non-magnetic fractions in relatively low volumes, and in order to be economic, need a central processing centre collecting fractions from up to 20 different sites. Stainless steel, aluminium, copper, lead and zinc, and non-metals need to be separated as far as possible – with the exception of aluminium it is difficult to economically separate the non-ferrous metals into discrete fractions by physical processing alone, although new research could change this, utilizing magnetic, photometric, electrostatic and conductivity/magnetic technologies[80].

A pre-concentrate can be obtained by screening which removes some of the non-metallics in the undersize (vibrating screens, rotating screens, bar sizers). The non-metallic fraction has become more important and currently is a major disposal concern and cost element. In West Germany (1990) the non-metallic fraction amounted to 470 000 tpa, at a cost of around 100 DM (approximately £34) per ton of disposal[80].

Rising current separation can be used to separate more of the non-metals by helping to liberate them and floating them off, or alternatively rotary air drum classifiers could be utilized. The application of jigs and other gravity separation techniques appears to be limited as they can only treat finer fractions and require large amounts of water[80].

After the majority of the non-metals have been removed, heavy media separation can be used to first separate any remaining non-metallics (heavy media at s.g 2.3-2.6), and to then separate aluminium, along with stones and glass (about 15% by weight) from the heavy metallics (heavy media at s.g 3.0). The size range of feed to the heavy media drum separators is between 6 to 150 mm, and recovers metal concentrates of up to 90% metal content. Alternatively, both water-only and heavy media hydrocyclones can be used, although the feed size is limited to minus 50 mm[80].

The aluminium concentrate can be further enriched by the use of eddy current separators to remove the remaining glass and stone. As an alternative to heavy media separation, it may be possible to use eddy current separators directly after rising current separation, giving four fractions: ferrous metals; non-metals; heavy non-ferrous metals; and aluminium.

3.4.1 UNITED STATES BUREAU OF MINES PROCESSES

In the late 1960s the United States Bureau of Mines began to develop unit operations and processes to treat autoshredder rejects - they investigated air classification, water elutriation, magnetic separation, hand picking, heavy media separation, cryogenics and liquation. Complete recovery of copper and other metals was economically made by hand and tool dismantling, leaching or selective melting of starters and generators. USBM also investigated plastic recovery and waste tyre treatment[43].

USBMs greatest difficulty to be resolved by applied research was how to adequately recover non-ferrous values from the non-magnetic reject. At the time, despite being extremely inefficient, hand sorting was the only method being used. Many old but proven mineral dressing techniques such as roasting, jigging, tabling, crushing, air and water classification or elutriation, magnetic, gravity and sink-float separations, screening, flotation, selective melting, leaching, etc. were applied to the relatively new problem of recovering valuable materials from automobile scrap. Also relatively new techniques were evaluated, including cryogenics and magnetic fluids[43].

After hand sorting, most non-ferrous metals were discarded as only the larger pieces of red (copper and brass) and white (zinc die case and aluminium) metals could be recovered. Only 14% of red metals and 28% of white metals could be recovered by hand picking. This led engineers at USBM to develop a flowsheet proposal for non-ferrous recovery using mechanical sorting (Figure 60). Air classification was used initially to separate light from heavy materials - air classification was used because of its operating simplicity and efficient removal of water-absorbing materials. This stage was followed by a screening operation to remove the fines. The oversize was then treated in a water elutriator to remove essentially all the non-metallics from the concentrate. The metal concentrate was then subjected to magnetic separation, from which there was a magnetic concentrate and a non-magnetic product which went to a hand picking stage to remove red metals. This was followed by a heavy medium separation to separate the zinc die cast from the aluminium in a water-galena slurry, although for an industrial process ferrosilicon would be used[43].

For the above process, the recovery of metal after air and water classification was approximately 87 weight percent. The main losses were of aluminium and copper in trim and coated wire (insulated wire approximate s.g = 3). Jigging of the light fraction produced a mixed metal concentrate of approximately 82% metal at 80% recovery. The detailed metal recoveries from this process were: Copper (and alloys) 39%; aluminium 53%; iron 96%; and zinc die cast 98%. The process was claimed in 1975 to be economic with high returns on investment[43,48].

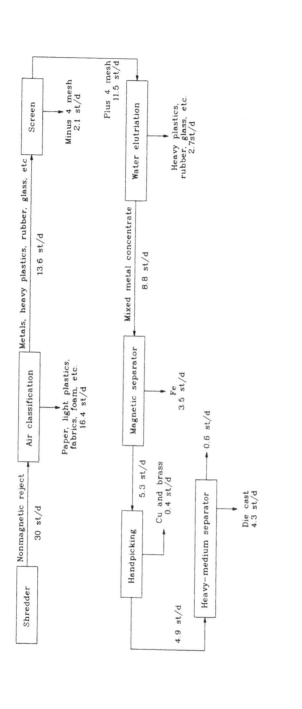

FIGURE 60. Non-ferrous recovery using mechanical sorting – adapted from reference 43

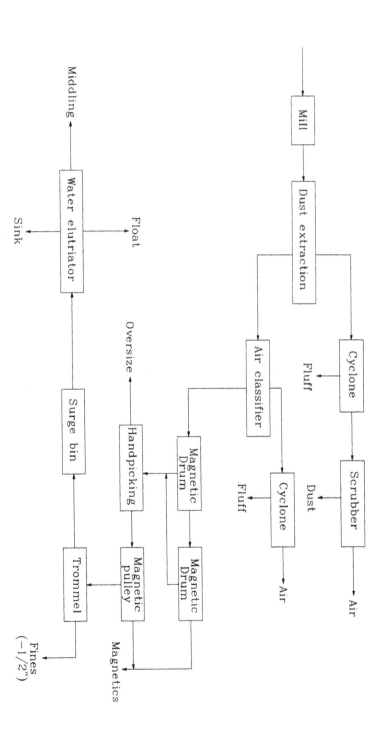

FIGURE 61. Low capital cost recovery system – adapted from reference 81

Preliminary research indicated that the eventual choice of flowsheet would have to be based on local variables, and so several other flowsheets were devised and the effectiveness of rising current separation was compared with heavy media separation - after upgrading to 75% metal content in an air classifier, water classification obtained a 98.7% concentrate at 95.5% recovery and HMS obtained a 99.1% concentrate at 98.9% recovery. The two flowsheets devised were: For low capital cost - air classification, magnetic separation, rising current separation, and hand sorting; and for optimum recovery (Figure 61) - air classification, magnetic separation, HMS at s.g. 2.65, HMS at s.g. 3.0, hand sorting and cryogenic crushing[43,81,82].

The air classifier used in the flowsheets was developed by USBM with a maximum capacity of 16 ton/hour, and was able to increase metal content up to 75% with recovery of over 95%. Both a vertical and a horizontal air classifier were developed - the vertical air classifier for removal of very light components and the horizontal for recovery of heavier components[27,43,83].

USBM installed their own design water elutriator at a shredder operator to test its feasibility. The operator showed a 34% increase in non-magnetic metals recovery over one year of operation as compared to recoveries from a previously used air classification system, despite not being used over the winter because of freezing conditions although this would not be such a problem in Europe and the United Kingdom in particular. The elutriator (Figure 25) had a capacity of 10 ton/hour and produced a 93.7% concentrate with a recovery of 93.1%[84].

Neither jigging nor tabling produced satisfactory metal recoveries or high purity products when used to separate aluminium from copper and zinc. Hence USBM developed a heavy media step at s.g 3.0 (Figure 62). For separation of zinc from the remaining non-ferrous concentrate cryogenic crushing was investigated, chilling to -30°C embrittles the zinc and it can be separated from

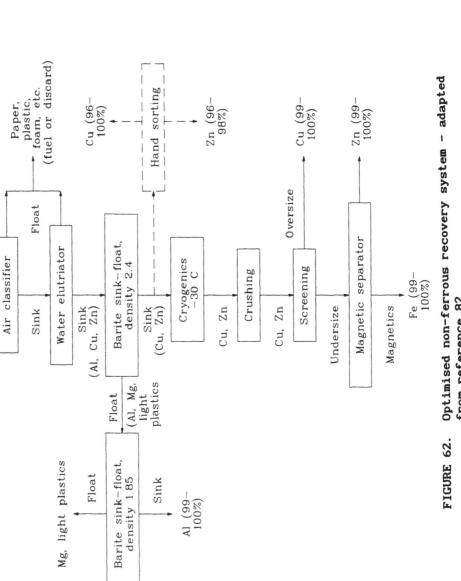

FIGURE 62. Optimised non-ferrous recovery system – adapted from reference 82

the remaining ductile metals (e.g. copper) by crushing and screening[27,45,81].

3.4.2 OTHER PROCESSES

There are many different processes which have been based, to a greater or lesser degree, on the pioneering work carried out by USBM, some of which will be described here. Some of the processes are simple shredding - windsifting - magnetic separation processes, others are much more complex procedures which try to get as many discrete products as possible.

Lindemann have developed a process based on the 1450 kW Shredder Plant. This is a dry shredder which has two explosion-proof dust extraction plants - one connected to the fragmentizer and the other to the separating drum. Separation of the shredded scrap from non-metallic contamination if effected by sucking-off at the fragmentizer housing as well as in the succeeding windsifter drum. The separating drum is followed by magnetic separation (magnetic drum separator). It is necessary at present to manually pick from the sorting belt after magnetic separation, to remove pieces of steel which are still connected to copper, for example starter motors, wiper motors, etc.[74]. Another Lindemann plant is shown in Figure 63, the Zerdirator, which uses the same technology as above[42,44].

Ferro Met Inc. in Etiwanda, California had to devise a new system which did not pollute the air due to strict pollution controls (1979). Originally an air separation system was used to upgrade the non-magnetic rejects from 10% to 50% non-ferrous metals, which would then be sold to specialist companies for further separation. Apart from the air pollution, air systems also had the following disadvantages: they consume large amounts of electricity; the size of ducts makes them hazardous and costly to maintain; there are chain reaction explosions from fumes which fill the fragmentizer, ducts and cyclones and hot metals sometimes

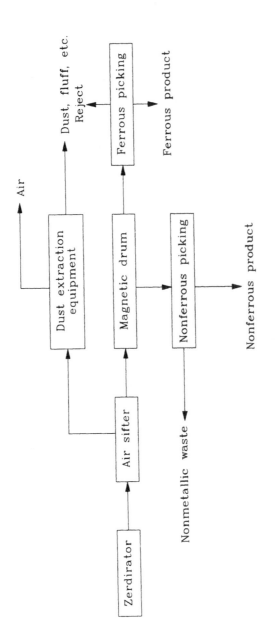

FIGURE 63. The Lindemann Zerdirator plant - adapted from reference 44

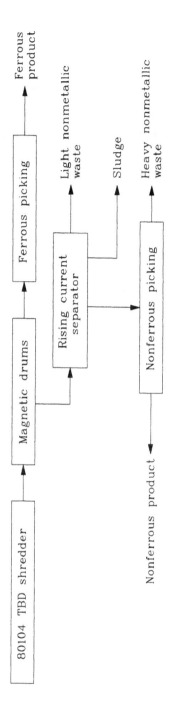

FIGURE 64. The Newell wet shredding system

ignite fires in residue piles. The new, simple method used to eliminate the need for air cleaning equipment was to use a wet shredding system with carefully metered water and controlled conveyor and magnetic drum speeds. The water reduces the temperature so that fumes do not form and eliminates fire and air pollution and makes explosions less frequent and less damaging. The fluff is heavier, due to the contained water, which helps in making the magnetic separation more efficient as the magnetic drum pulls the ferrous metals away from the non-magnetics. Wet shredding has reduced production delays by 25% because of the loss of the air cleaning system, and also reduced power consumption and non-ferrous metal losses. The main disadvantage with the system as used in this example is that the non-ferrous residue is only 10% metals, which is too low to sell, although this problem could easily be overcome with the installation of a rising current separator[78].

A wet shredding system has also been developed by Newell Industries Ltd. (Figure 64). This consists of a wet fragmentizer followed by magnetic drum separators and a rising current separator to remove the non-ferrous metals from the non-magnetic fraction. Any remaining magnetics are removed from this fraction by an overband magnetic separator. It is now possible to follow the Newell Wet Shredding System immediately with a Non-ferrous (eddy current) Separator without the need for heavy medium separation[41,85].

Since 1970 a growing proportion of shredder residue has been shipped to central processing plants. The metals contained in the residue are mainly zinc and aluminium, with smaller amounts of copper, stainless steel and lead. The use of die cast zinc parts is decreasing and it is becoming less important, but at the same time the aluminium content of scrapped cars is increasing and becoming more important, this is a desirable chain of events as aluminium can be separated relatively easily from impurities by the use of eddy current separators. The residue is usually subjected to two stages of HMS using drums or cyclones. The first stage of HMS is usually to float materials with specific gravities of less than 2.4 (plastic and rubber, for example) and the second stage is generally to float materials with specific gravities from 2.4 to 3.0 (aluminium, stone and glass). The lightest fraction goes to landfill, the aluminium fraction can be treated by eddy current separation, and the heavy fraction is subjected to hand picking and sweating. The whole process from scrapped automobiles to end products is shown in Figure 65[1,13].

Venti Oelde produce systems to recover metal concentrates from fragmentizer residues. Their HM 8000 system is unusual in that it includes heavy media separation for single shredders as small as 2000 HP. After windsifting, which upgrades metal content to 85%, there is a screening stage followed by rubber separation using Vibrosort - a Venti Oelde developed vibratory sorter. The residue is then washed and subjected to two stages of HMS to separate into a non-metal fraction, an aluminium fraction and a heavy metals fraction[86,87].

Following is a description of a typical shredder plant in Duisburg, Germany. The non-magnetic fraction (50% metal content) is screened at 8 mm. The plus 8 mm is sent to the HMS plant of Metal Float GmbH which has a throughput of 2-4 ton/hour. Ferrosilicon is used as the heavy medium in a two-compartment drum separator. The minus 8 mm fraction is sent to the SMA-plant (Figure 66), the total capacity of which is 1.0-1.5 ton/hour. The aluminium fraction (obtained from the sinks of a rising current separator and the top product of a jig) is ground in an impact breaker for separation of glass and stone (up to 40% weight). The heavy metal concentrate, bottom product from the jig, is then sent for thermal treatment[80].

The heavy media plant at Eumet GmbH, Frankfurt, Germany has a capacity of up to 25 ton/hour (Figure 67). The metal recovery is

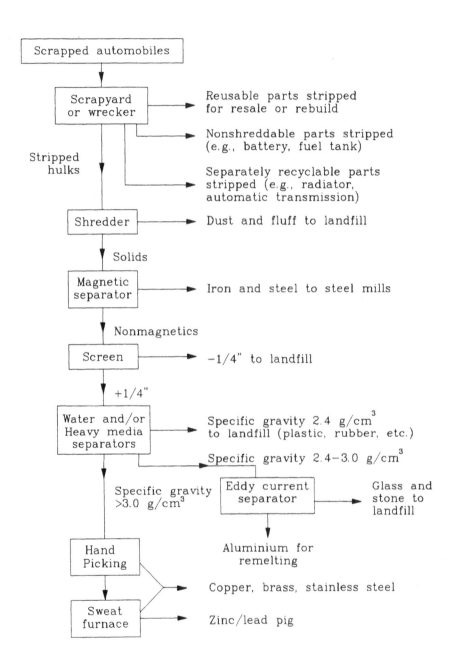

FIGURE 65.   The processing of scrapped automobiles

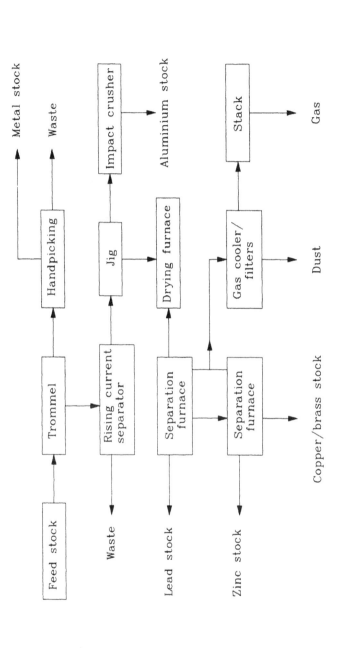

FIGURE 66. The SMA process plant – adapted from reference 80

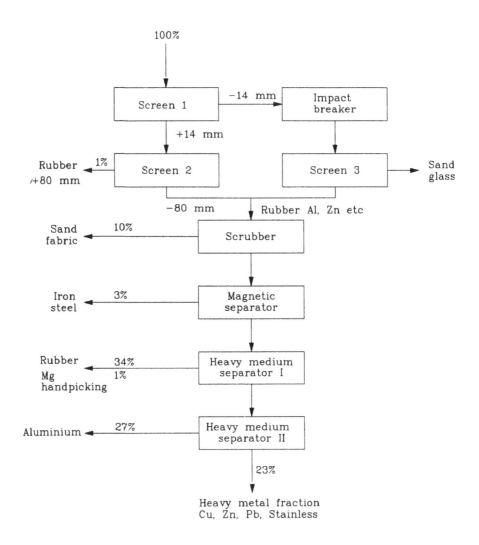

FIGURE 67.   Heavy medium plant – adapted from reference 73

approximately 95%, for a ferrosilicon loss of around 4-5 kg per ton of feed. A two-compartment drum separator is used: separation of rubber and magnesium at s.g 2.2, the rubber fraction is usually discarded but some cement plants are able to use it as fuel; separation of aluminium at s.g 3.4. Instead of dumping, the non-magnetic fines are treated by a process for recovery of non-ferrous metals using shaking table, jigs, etc. Another German heavy media plant is Metallhuttenwerke Bruch KG in Dortmund. This plant is especially used for the recovery of aluminium - heavy media separation at s.g 2.5 and again at s.g 2.9[73,80].

There are several types of HMS system - for relatively constant feed composition the two-compartment drum is one of the most versatile. The drum is divided into high and low gravity fractions, each filled with ferrosilicon suspension in water. The feed enters the low density section where the organics float and the metals sink and are transferred by lifters to the high density section. Here the aluminium floats and the copper, zinc and stainless steel sink. All of the products are discharged onto screens where the media drains off. Water sprays are used to wash off any ferrosilicon particles remaining on products and special closed loop cleaning circuits recover and clean the water and ferrosilicon for re-use. Heavy media separation can be further improved to separate heavy metals from one another by the use of magnetic levitation. Pilot plants with capacities of up to 1.5 ton/hour for feed sizes of plus 0.1 mm minus 30 mm have been built in Czechoslovakia, the United Kingdom, Japan, USSR, Israel and the United States, but no full scale industrial plants have been reported using magnetic fluids[78,80].

Hydrocyclones which are water-only or heavy media fed can be used for sink-float operations as well. The feed is shredder residue of size range minus 50 mm plus 0.5 mm and can be separated into separate fractions by specific gravity by the use of only one heavy medium suspension. Water-only hydrocyclones are used to

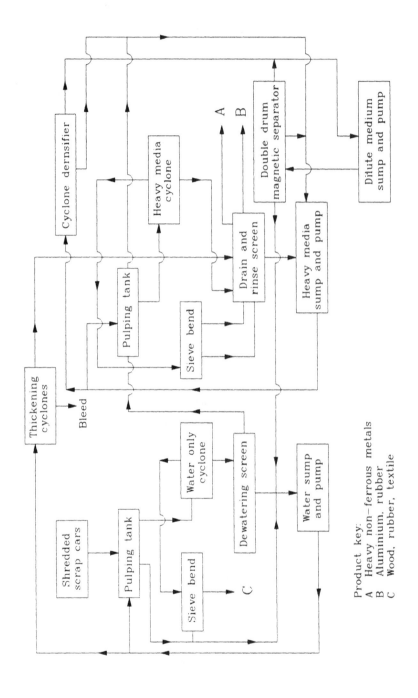

Product key:
A Heavy non-ferrous metals
B Aluminium, rubber
C Wood, rubber, textile

FIGURE 68.   Cyclone separation plant – adapted from reference 89

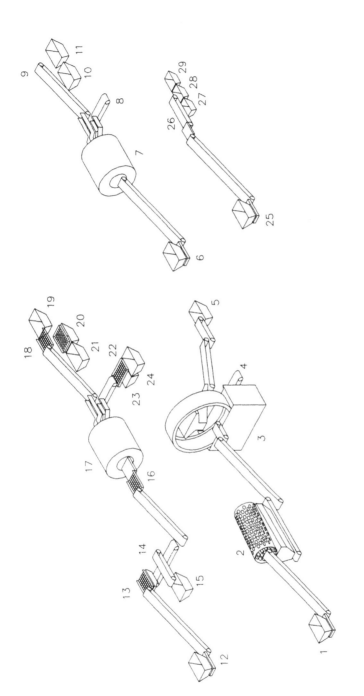

FIGURE 69. Shredder rejects separation plant – adapted from reference 90

separate below s.g 2.6 because this fraction may contain a large proportion of porous materials which would absorb the heavy medium.   After this stage a heavy medium cyclone process can be used at s.g 2.8.   The first cyclone plant of this kind was built in Holland in 1977 and the first to be operated in the United States was built in 1981 (Figure 68).   The Dutch plant treats 7 ton/hour feed (containing 5 ton/hour metals) and the American plant treats 25 ton/hour feed (containing on average 6 ton/hour metals).   This plant (Reclamation and Recycling Division, Reynolds Metals Co., Sheffield, Alabama) has an annual output of 30 000 tons non-ferrous metals.   The shredder residue is screened in a trommel at 2", the oversize being reshredded and returned to the trommel.   Water-only cyclones treat the undersize to remove wood, rubber and textiles and the underflow is then treated by the primary HM cyclones that remove the heavy metals.   The overflow from the primary HM cyclone is further treated to obtain a clean aluminium concentrate in secondary hydrocyclones.   The heavy medium is a mixture of magnetite and ferrosilicon and the plant can also be used to treat shredded MSW[7,88,89].

A state-of-the-art non-ferrous separation plant is operated by Dunn Brothers (Metals) Ltd., in Birmingham, England (Figure 69).   The feed consists of non-magnetic autoshredder rejects (1) from various fragmentizers, which is trommel screened at 100 mm (2).   A rising current separator (3) is used to wash off the light non-metallics (4), the sinks (5) being removed by a rotary lifter[90].

The sinks from the wash plant are transferred to a primary heavy medium plant (6-7), where a separation is effected at s.g 2.4-2.6, the floats consisting of heavy non-metallics (8).   The sinks comprise a metal concentrate with glass and stone impurities which are passed over a magnetic pulley to produce a ferrous concentrate (10) and a non-ferrous pre-concentrate (11)[90].

The non-ferrous pre-concentrate is transferred to the

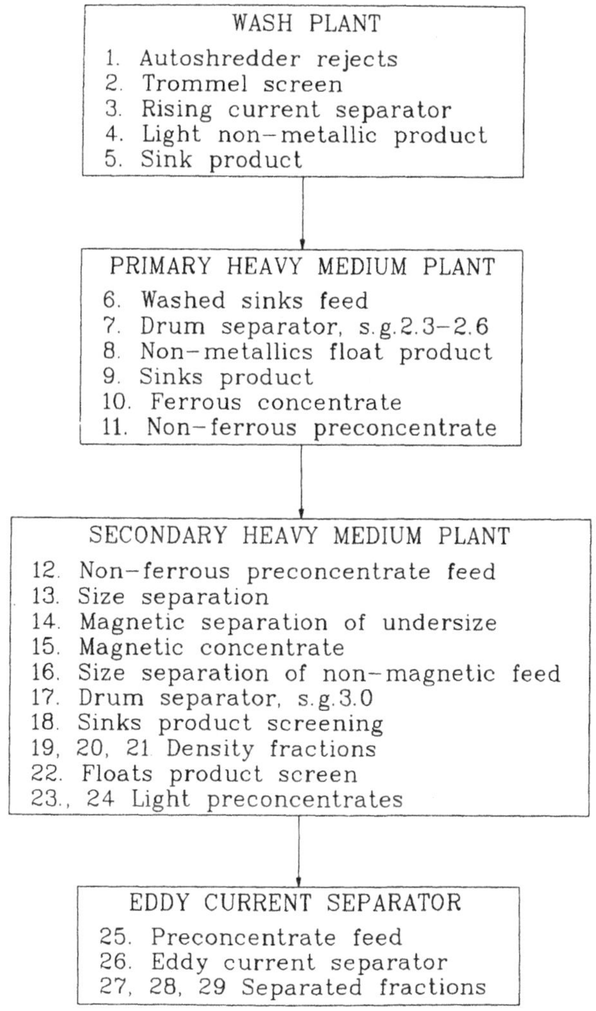

WASH PLANT

1. Autoshredder rejects
2. Trommel screen
3. Rising current separator
4. Light non—metallic product
5. Sink product

PRIMARY HEAVY MEDIUM PLANT

6. Washed sinks feed
7. Drum separator, s.g.2.3—2.6
8. Non—metallics float product
9. Sinks product
10. Ferrous concentrate
11. Non—ferrous preconcentrate

SECONDARY HEAVY MEDIUM PLANT

12. Non—ferrous preconcentrate feed
13. Size separation
14. Magnetic separation of undersize
15. Magnetic concentrate
16. Size separation of non—magnetic feed
17. Drum separator, s.g.3.0
18. Sinks product screening
19, 20, 21 Density fractions
22. Floats product screen
23., 24 Light preconcentrates

EDDY CURRENT SEPARATOR

25. Preconcentrate feed
26. Eddy current separator
27, 28, 29 Separated fractions

FIGURE 70. Shredder rejects separation plant

secondary heavy medium plant (12-17).   Initially there is a size separation (13) - a mixed metal concentrate is recovered here (the only large particles remaining are metals as the remaining non-metallics consist of brittle glass and stone).   The undersize is subjected to another magnetic separation stage (14) which produces another magnetic concentrate from the remaining unrecovered ferrous metals.   The non-magnetics are passed over a vibratory screen to remove the very fine undersize (16 - the subsequent stage of heavy medium separation operates at near to its maximum density and any fines entering would cause an undesirable increase in medium viscosity).   The heavy medium drum separator (17) separates at s.g 3.0.   The sinks consist of a heavy metal concentrate which is passed over a double deck vibratory screen (18) to produce three different bulk density products (19, 20, 21), and the floats consist of an aluminium alloy concentrate (85 wt%) with glass and stone impurities which is screened (22) to give two different pre-concentrates (23, 24)[90].

Either the product 23 or the product 24 is transferred to a Newell non-ferrous eddy current separator (26) for cleaning of the aluminium alloy concentrate, giving a ferrous fraction (27), a waste fraction (28) and an aluminium alloy concentrate (29)[90].

3.5 SUMMARY

There have been many significant technical advances in the processing of fragmentized metals wastes over the past three decades.   Efficient, modern process plants now make an important contribution to the amount of recycled ferrous and non-ferrous scrap particularly from redundant automobiles.   There are still technical advances to be made for further improvement of separation processes, but an influential factor in the future may be manufacturers efforts to deliberately design automobiles for easier and more efficient dismantling for recycling of component materials.

CHAPTER FOUR

THE PROCESSING OF GRANULATED METAL WASTES

There are a large number of items that require finer shredding than is possible with fragmentizers, in order to liberate values, including cable and wire (power lines, telephone cables containing copper and aluminium conductors with rubber, plastic, paper and cloth insulators which may be moist or slightly greasy); electrical equipment (small motors, relays, etc.); power plugs; telephone exchange equipment; electronic equipment (hi-fi units, televisions, video recorders, computers, etc.); lamp sockets, neon tubes; tyres; inner tube valves; aluminium joinery sections (with heat insulation); bottle screw caps; toothpaste tubes; tin cans aluminium foil, etc.[91,92,93]. These types of material are processed through granulators, and although such operations are not carried out on the same scale as autoshredding, they represent a very important source for recovery of valuable materials, for example there are around 20 million rubber tyres discarded in the United Kingdom per annum; 7 million lbs of obsolete military electronic hardware discarded in the United States and 1.5 billion lbs of insulated wire produced per annum in the United States[7,92,94].

Most granulation processes are designed to deal with one particular type of scrap, although they tend to be fairly flexible in terms of the feed received. Unlike autoshredding a number of granulator processes need to produce clean non-metallic concentrates as well as metal concentrates in order to be economical. Granulators are ideal for in-house recycling, for example, of the 1.5 billion lbs of insulated copper wire produced per year in the United States 4% is defective and recycled in-house[7].

There are various techniques for stripping insulation from wire and cable, mechanical stripping (abrasion or shearing); thermal stripping (high temperature or low temperature); chemical stripping; and combinations of these methods.

Resilient items, such as auto tyres, respond better to shearing and tearing machines than to impact type mills. For the treatment of large, complex, electronic scrap units shear-type shredders are also preferable as hammermills tend to bundle up steel and roll aluminium into egg shapes which leads to entrainment of impurities and (in the case of non-ferrous metals) reduces the susceptibility to eddy current separation (although the more regular shape will lead to improved gravity separation). The Cutler shredder, developed by AMG Resources, Birmingham, England, uses a novel attrition shearing action to produce an easily detinned steel shredded product from used cans. It consists of a contra-rotating cage and impeller, used cans are fed into the shredder and the cyclone created impels the tightly packed cans together. The paint and lacquer are stripped and scraped by repeated collisions and the fragments shear each other, thereby liberating the various fractions[32,95,96].

4.1 METAL RECLAMATION PROCESSES

(i) *United States Bureau of Mines Processes.* USBM has developed several processes for the recovery of values from scrap electronic equipment. These include shredding, wire picking, air classification, screening, magnetic separation, electrostatic separation, eddy current separation and additional treatments to give clean fractions of magnetics, aluminium alloys, copper alloys, austenitic stainless steels and non-metals from shredded electronic scrap[94].

Much of the research and development work was performed on

obsolete military electronic scrap. In addition to engineering metals such as copper and aluminium, this scrap also contained significant amounts of gold and silver and the precious metals mainly presented in three fractions: air classifier lights: wire bundles; and the high tension concentrate (68-97%) of the gold and 76-98% of the silver. The importance of recovering this precious metal fraction is illustrated by the fact that in the United States 79% of gold and 38% of silver are recycled. It is estimated that 29% of gold and silver consumption is accounted for by the electronic industries, so it is important that obsolete scrap be treated for recovery of precious metals. Recovery of these metals from electronic scrap is difficult due to the complexity and heterogeneity of circuits and components. Precious metals are used in components such as pin connectors, contact points, silver coated wire, terminals, capacitors, plugs and relays. It the scrap is initially upgraded to recover aluminium, nickel and other base metals, then the quantity of materials to process for precious metals recovery is reduced. This leads to lower toll charges for the same amount of precious metal, and reduced penalty for contained nickel[96,97].

USBM set up a Process Research Unit (PRU) which was capable of treating 500 lbs of avionic scrap an hour (Figure 71). The process comprised a 25 HP hammermill comminution section which was followed by air classification, wire picking, magnetic drum separation and sizing. The magnetic fraction was trommel screened and the non-magnetic fraction vibratory screened. The preceding process was continuous and it was followed by a batch process on the non-magnetic product, consisting of a magnetic pre-clean, eddy current separation and high tension separation. The products from this process, which worked very well on heterogeneous scrap, were an iron base fraction which could be used to cement copper, and then precious metals and nickel could be recovered from the residue; a mixed metal fraction; a wire fraction; air classifier

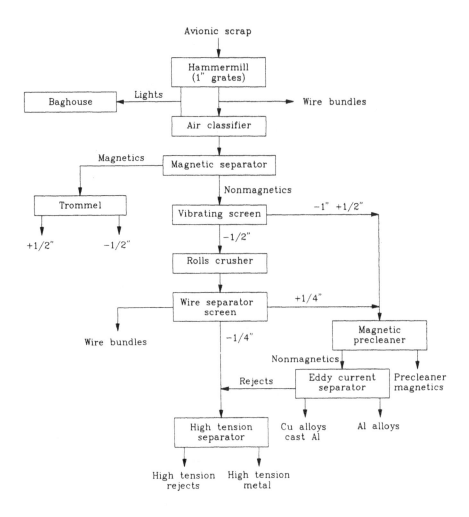

FIGURE 71.   Mechanical processing of avionic scrap

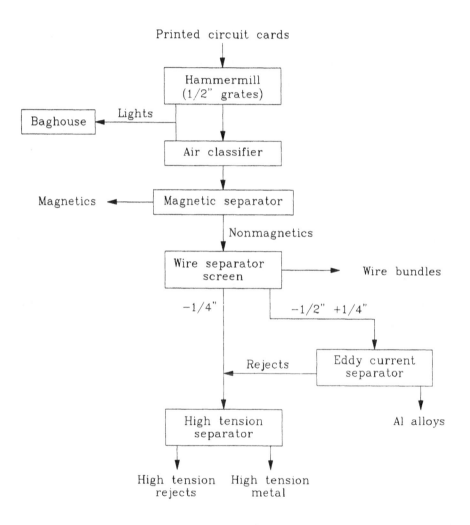

FIGURE 72. Mechanical processing of printed circuit boards

lights; aluminium and copper concentrates. Another similar process has also been developed specifically for use on printed circuit boards (Figure 72)[96,97].

(ii) Other processes. Warren Spring Laboratory (WSL) developed a process flowsheet for the recovery of fine fragmentizer waste which would otherwise have been discarded, rather than processed further, and although no fine comminution was used to obtain liberation, the process employed the same type of operations as a granulator circuit (Figure 73). Following a divergator, a type of vibrating rod grizzly, the undersize material was subjected to air classification. The light fraction passed to a jigging section where the non-metallics formed a top product and were discarded. Both the concentrate and the undersize (-2.0 mm) were passed over magnetic separators to give a ferrous and a non-ferrous concentrate. The heavy fraction from the air classifier was immediately passed over a magnetic separator to obtain a ferrous concentrate. The non-magnetic fraction was a low grade non-ferrous concentrate which was passed through a roll crusher. Screening removed ductile non-ferrous metals in the oversize, and discarded the brittle non-metallics in the undersize[40].

A French company, Le Comptoir Industriel des Metaux et Plastiques (CIMP), produce mechanical equipment for the recovery of metals contained in insulating materials, such as scrap electric cable and wire, plug and socket connectors, and electrical or electronic components. Plant is available to reclaim aluminium (Figure 74), copper (Figure 75), alloys and clean plastic materials at outputs of up to 2 tonnes/hour. The processes are very similar and based on a standard process designed for processing scrap cable and wire (Figure 76). This consists of a primary granulator (A), a pneumatic conveyor (B), a secondary granulator (C), a pneumatic conveyor (D), and a density separator (air table - E). The granulator has a 75 HP motor and blades with a special profile and can handle up to 2 tonne/hour.

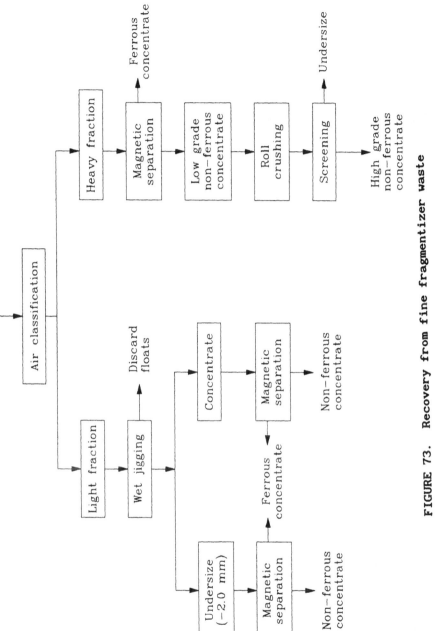

FIGURE 73. Recovery from fine fragmentizer waste

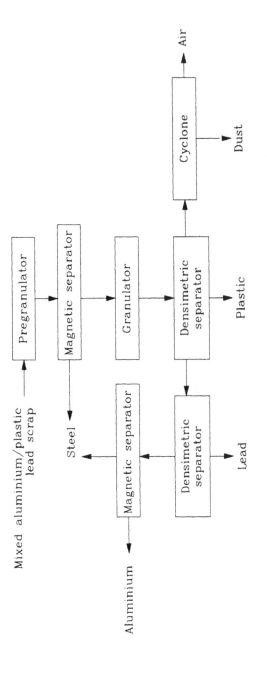

FIGURE 74. Aluminium processing plant layout

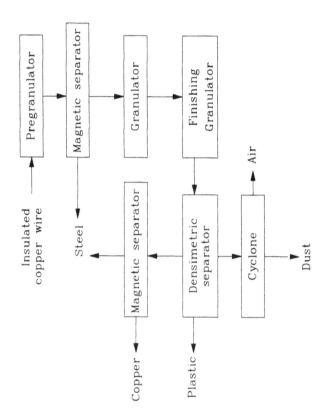

FIGURE 75. Copper processing plant layout

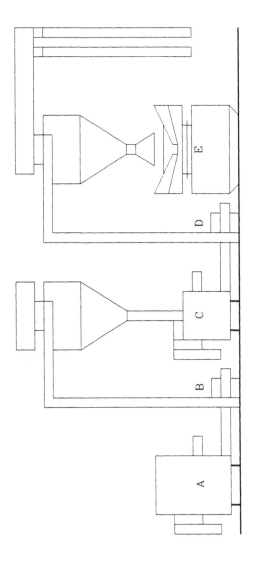

FIGURE 76. Granulator layout (CIMP)

The plant has 98% metal recovery at 99% purity and can be used to process fine cables, cables wrapped in fabric or paper, and wet cables. There are several different modular units which can be added to processes to suit a particular feed, such as magnetic separators and pre-granulators with capacities up to 5 tonnes/hour[91].

Several companies produce systems similar to CIMP. System Redoma produce a compact turn-key plant which can be extended to suit the feed with extra granulators, rough choppers, proportional feeding and extra magnetic separation[98]. E. Laursens Maskinfabrik produce Eldan recycling plant which can recover up to 99% aluminium from electrical scrap cable and are modular for flexibility to meet the requirements needed for processing different feeds. A super chopper is available which can reduce 10-15 tonnes/hour of light scrap, including white goods, tyres, tables, etc. The standard process consists of a rasper, an overband magnetic separator, a granulator, a three-deck PVC separator and a gravity separator that can obtain metal purities of up to 99%. Cable stripping equipment is available for cable up to 150 mm diameter at rates of 30 m per minute[99]. Scandinavian Recycling AB produce equipment to convert electrical, electronic, and cable scrap, and the non-ferrous fraction from autoshredders into ferrous, light copper, heavy copper and aluminium concentrates. The most unusual feature of these plants is the use of a drum wind separator[100].

A cable scrap processing plant with an output of 6000 tonnes/year has been built in Bytom, Poland, as a result of co-operation between Scandinavian Recycling and Kusakovsky Companies. It accepts all types of dry cable scrap; copper; aluminium; lead; iron; tinplate; zinc coat; lead shields; steel strip reinforcement; and different types of insulating materials: plastics; rubber; textiles. The process consists of four stage comminution, two stage air separation and screen classification

(Figure 77). A 250 tonne pressing and cutting machine cuts the cable into 100-500 mm long segments, the products of which are hand picked on a sorting belt (to remove massive steel pieces in the form of grips and joints). The second comminution stage is a slow speed cutting fragmentizer, with a 50 mm bar screen. The output from the fragmentizer is magnetically separated to remove steel and reinforced cable. The main scrap processing stage consists of two identical granulation and separation lines, each with two granulation stages and a separating table. The first stage of granulation reduces the scrap to 10-1/mm which is then magnetically separated - the non-magnetics are then granulated again to 3-8 mm. This final stage of comminution is followed by air table separation. The middlings from the air tables are returned to the second granulation stage and the light fraction is screened to give a fine metallic concentrate (-0.8 mm fraction is 70-80% metal) and a waste fraction. If the feed comprises both copper and aluminium a final air table can be used to obtain a copper granulate and an aluminium granulate[101].

Electrostatic separation can be used for plastic/metal separation after granulation. It is also possible to obtain total metallic removal from other non-conductors, such as ceramics, provided there is a sufficient degree of liberation. The usual process route is to pass the middling product of an air table over a screen to remove the oversize. This leaves a middlings consisting of about 60% metal which can be upgraded using high tension separation to give a 99% metallic concentrate at 90% recovery. High tension separation can also be used to obtain a clean plastic concentrate, less than 0.1% metal, from a mixture of 5% metal/95% plastic.

Carpco Inc., of Florida, United States, produce electrostatic equipment especially for this purpose where the wire is coarse chopped at 5" and then granulated to -¼" (Figure 78). Carpco also have a similar process for recovering aluminium, PET and HDPE from

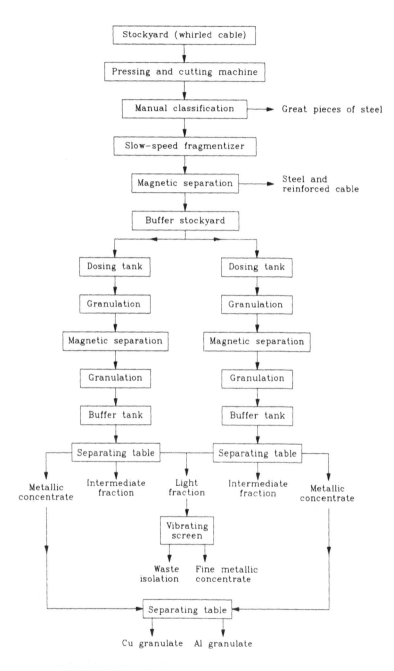

FIGURE 77.   Cable processing plant

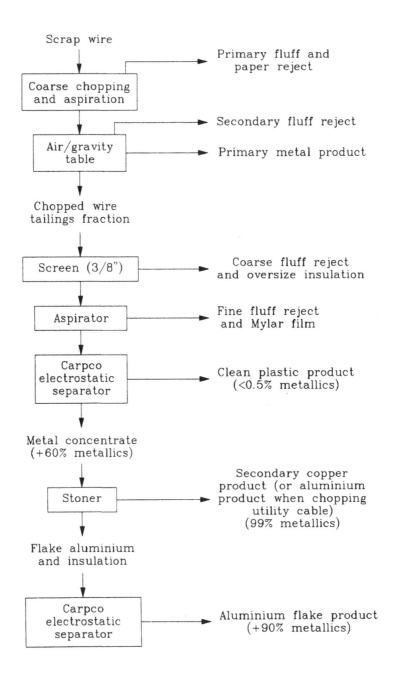

FIGURE 78.   Scrap wire processing (Carpco)

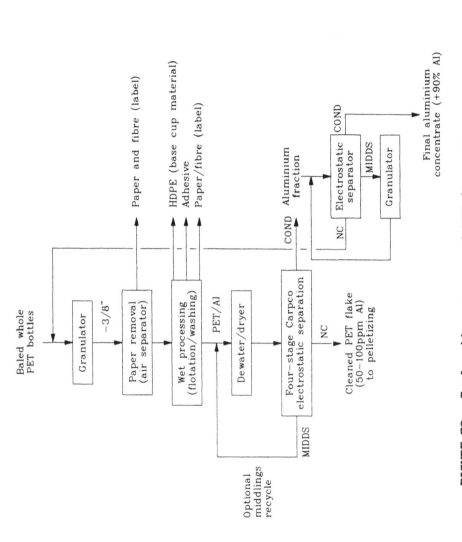

FIGURE 79. Reclamation of chopped PET (Carpco)

chopped PET bottles at feed rates of 2000 lbs/hour - Figure 79. Bales of PET bottles are granulated to below $\frac{3}{8}$" and are passed over an air separator, a water elutriator, dried, and then passed finally over different combinations of electrostatic separators[102,103,104,105,106].

4.2 WASTE TYRE PROCESSING

Automobile and commercial vehicle tyres are a special problem. Millions are discarded each year, and they cause a major disposal headache. They can rise to the surface in landfills, and in open air waste tyre stores in the United States, where there are 2-3 billion tyres stockpiled (1992) they are proving to be ideal breeding grounds for mosquitoes. Hence it is desirable to at least reduce the tyres to small granules of rubber before disposal, or preferably, to recycle the constituents as far as possible. A power plant in Wolverhampton, England, uses waste tyres as fuel, but there are several uses for rubber crumb produced in tyre shredding which should be introduced wherever possible - tyre shredding can also lead to the recovery of high grade steel scrap of near constant composition. Rubber crumb from reduced tyres can be used for sportsfield surfaces, safe playground surfaces, tiles for paved areas, hygienic animal mats, insulation tiles for underground railways, flooring for shooting galleries (to prevent ricochets), flooring for weights rooms, rubber slabs for railway crossings, etc[107,108,109].

Several companies make specialist equipment for tyre recycling. Shredtech manufacture a Tirecycler which reduces tyres to 1½" chips. Newell Engineering Ltd. produce a tyre shredder which incorporates contra-rotating cutters mounted in a quickly interchangeable cassette and the cutter tips can be replaced individually (Figure 80). Permanently installed hydraulic nuts ensure that the end load of the cutter assemblies is maintained under all conditions. The major cause of loss of performance is

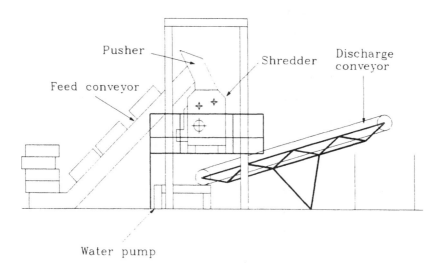

FIGURE 80. Tyre shredding plant (Newell)

the result of excessive clearance developing between cutter knives - the use of a hydraulic nut to maintain end load reduces this problem.   Both CIMP and Eldan Recycling Systems produce plant to recover the steel, rubber and fabric contained in waste tyres, as individual fractions (Figures 81 and 82)[91,99,110,111].

4.3 BATTERY PROCESSING

One of the major uses of lead is in lead-acid batteries, yet the amount of lead-acid battery recyclers has dwindled to only a few in number because of environmental regulations which have caused more problems than they have solved.   There are, however, several different physical processes for recovery of the lead.   In one an acid resistant shredder is used as the single stage of comminution (Figure 83).   It consists of two slow speed counter rotating crushing rolls with meshing disc shaped cutting tools which are fitted with staggered breaking teeth.   The discharge is neutralized and classified at 30 mm, the oversize being returned to the shredder.   Classification and desliming obtain a product which is treated in a water-only hydrocyclone, this gives an organic product and lead metal.   The slimes are thickened and filtered to give a lead oxide and a lead sulphate product.

In another process whole or shredded lead-acid batteries, together with a quantity of sodium carbonate and water, are fed continuously into a rotating drum separator containing grinding balls.   The battery fragments are broken up and degraded, the acid is neutralized and the lead sulphate precipitates to lead carbonate which forms a heavy medium suspension.   The organic floats and the active suspension overflow into a first trommel. The sinks consist of grid metal and battery parts of lower grade antimony lead alloy and are mechanically removed at the opposite end to a second trommel.   A proportion of the suspension is returned to the drum and the rest is thickened[112, 113].

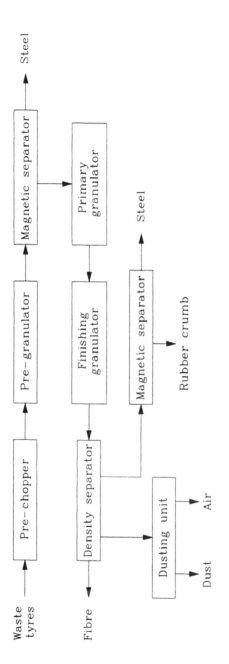

FIGURE 81. Tyre processing plant layout (CIMP)

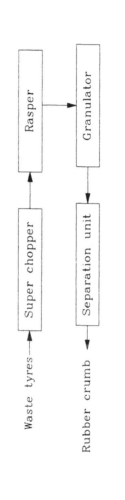

FIGURE 82. Modular shredding and granulation plants

4.4 THERMAL PROCESSING SYSTEMS

4.4.1 CRYOGENIC TREATMENT

In 1973 USBM reported the results of research on the use of cryogens to reclaim non-ferrous scrap metals. Liquid nitrogen, dry ice, and a mixture of dry ice and ethanol were used to aid in the separation of insulated wire, shredded automobile non-ferrous concentrates, small motors, generators, and scrap tyres[114].

Wire with PVC and neoprene insulation was chilled to -60°C and -195°C using different cryogens, roll crushed and subjected to water elutriation. Both low temperature processes yielded similar recoveries - the sink product was 99% metallic and the float product was 99% non-metallic[114].

Autoshredder non-ferrous concentrates containing zinc die-case alloys, copper, and aluminium were chilled to -72°C and reduced in a hammermill. The product from the hammermill was screened at 1" - the oversize contained 97.2% of the aluminium and 100% of the copper, and the undersize contained 100% of the cryogenically embrittled zinc (97% pure)[114].

Further work conducted by USBM concluded that cryogenic cooling could be beneficial in the processing of scrap tyres but not in the processing of generators, starters and small motors. Indirect chilling was found to be feasible and helped reduce loss of the cryogenic[43,114].

Air Products and Chemicals Inc. designed a process for recovery of copper and other metals from cryogenically chilled mixed scrap (Figure 84). Scrap containing high copper plus aluminium and zinc, precious metals may also be present, is processes including discarded automobile generators, voltage regulators, electric motors, armatures, stators, electrical wire, electronic devices, relays, etc. having high copper content, an appreciable aluminium content, organic insulating materials, ferrous metals and other metals. The feedstock is subjected to cryogenic cooling which embrittles ferrous metals and organic

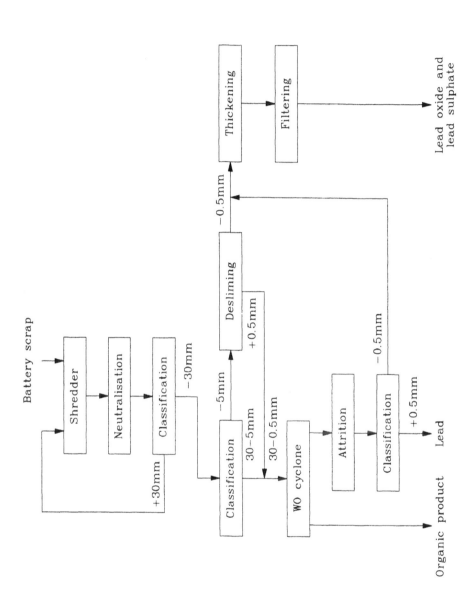

FIGURE 83. Battery processing plant

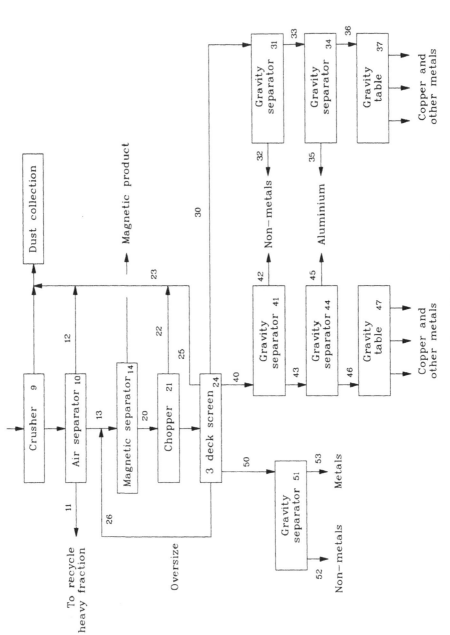

FIGURE 84. Cryogenic processing of mixed scrap

components, following which it is broken by impact and crushing. Air separation is used to separate into heavy and light fractions, the heavy fraction is magnetically separated and the non-magnetics are returned to the light fraction for further processing. The light fraction and heavy non-magnetics go to secondary crushing and this is followed by a secondary air separator and again the heavy fraction is magnetically separated. The non-magnetics are returned to the secondary crusher. The light fraction is reduced again in a tertiary comminution stage and magnetically separated. The non-magnetics go for further separation (process line 20 on Figure 84) to a granulator/wire chopper (21) because it has a high copper content which is ductile and not readily susceptible to impacting or crushing. A narrow size range is required so a shear action is needed to reduce the particles to minus ¼". The comminuted product is discharged to a three deck screen (24) - the plus ¼" fraction is recycled and the minus ¼" plus $\frac{1}{8}$" and the minus $\frac{1}{8}$" plus $\frac{1}{16}$" are both subjected to three stages of air separation to obtain non-metals, aluminium, copper and other metals. The minus $\frac{1}{16}$" fraction is treated by a single air table to separate the non-metals from the metals[115].

Another example of cryogenic treatment of electrical scrap is a process developed by Jeno Inc. in the USA, where the feed is conveyed to the entrance of a shaftless rotating drum with internal helical baffles - the material is continuously exposed to cryogenic coolant to be frozen and rendered brittle. The material is then ground in a mill and separated conventionally. Cryogenic processing can be used to selectively embrittle several different materials and after embrittlement the power requirements for size reduction are about one tenth of the power requirements at ambient temperatures[116,117].

Probably the most useful application of cryogenic grinding is in the embrittlement of tyres from which the rubber, the steel and the fabric can be reclaimed individually (Figure 85). However,

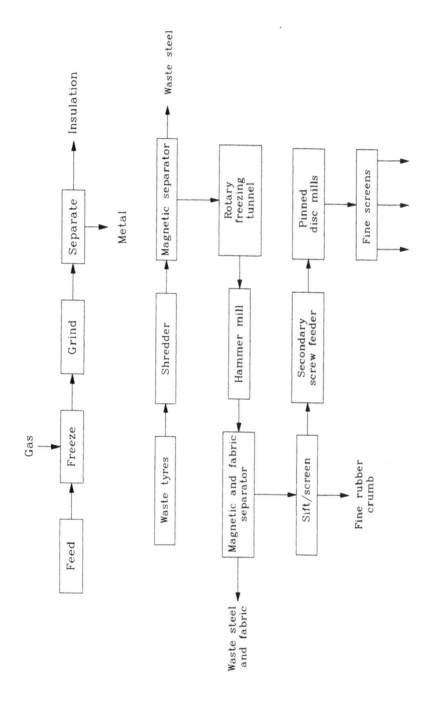

FIGURE 85. Cryogenic grinding plant

with the improvements in shredders and granulators for special feeds such as scrap tyres and wire scrap, it is unlikely that cryogenic processing will gain widespread acceptance as the economics have not been proven to be acceptable[92,93,117].

4.4.2 HOT CRUSHING

USBM devised a technique for separation of cast and wrought aluminium scrap which exploits their differences in hot ductility. It can be used to upgrade mixed aluminium scrap into high value, recyclable grades of wrought and cast alloys - mixed aluminium scrap cannot be used to produce wrought aluminium, only low value castings. The process consists of heating the scrap, fragmenting and screening[118].

4.4.3 THERMALLY ASSISTED LIBERATION

Research at the University of Birmingham has focused on the development of a low cost alternative to cryogenic embrittlement. Rather than freezing the feed, the metal bearing polymers are heated and then air quenched. Treatments of 250°C for thermoplastics and 300°C for thermosets result in a reduction in fracture toughness and a significant increase in grindability without emission of large quantities of fume. Subsequent ball milling and screening produces a relatively clean metallic oversize which can be used as feed for a secondary smelter. The minus 1 mm fraction contains about 15% copper which can be recovered by high tension separation[45,119].

4.5 SUMMARY

As with the processing of fragmentized metal wastes, there have been significant technical advances in separation methods applied to granulated wastes. Current research is aimed at developing new and improved means of separating increasingly complex mixtures of metals and alloys[145].

CHAPTER FIVE

THE PROCESSING OF URBAN WASTE

The processing of municipal solid waste (MSW) to recover materials
is both technically and economically difficult. Urban waste is
low in grade in comparison to other secondary material sources,
highly heterogeneous, and of constantly changing composition (both
day-to-day, season-to-season, and region-to-region). Technology
does exist to obtain adequate separation of the component
materials, but in many instances the cost of recovery exceeds the
revenue from the reclaimed materials. Thus processing of MSW for
materials recovery could more usefully be seen as a waste disposal
alternative rather than as a profit-making venture - although in
the long term there appears to be no practical alternative to the
present high costs of refuse disposal without recycling[20].

Out of over 20 million tons/year of MSW in the United
Kingdom, more than 90% is sent to landfill, the only other common
form of waste disposal being incineration in major connurbations.
In the United States 115 million tons/year go to landfill and 30
million tons/year are incinerated. The disposal practices used
for large quantities of consumer waste result in a substantial
loss of both resources and energy, and contribute to air, land and
water pollution. The disposal problems of most countries are
increasing significantly, not only because of rapidly increasing
populations, but also because affluence and packaging techniques
increase per capita waste production. Open cast dumping and
controlled/sanitary landfilling have been superficially the most
attractive disposal techniques from an economic point of view, but
now in some places land and transport costs have become
prohibitive. Incineration is an alternative, this process reduces
bulk but extremely strict air cleaning is required. It is ironic

147

that pollution controls can reduce some recycling, air pollution control encourages a move away from incineration where at least some energy and material can be recycled.   The practice of salvaging from landfills is dying out as well, as access to landfills is denied due to public hygiene regulations[6,20,24].

One of the largest barriers to recycling of MSW is that waste disposal used to be purely a local government problem in the United Kingdom, and there was no industry input to provide finance for the development, technology and competition necessary, although this may change with the introduction of private tendering for waste disposal[6].

Ideally all waste should be separated at source, but unfortunately this leads to very inefficient collection and requires total compliance by the waste producer; collection efficiency has to be optimised – in the UK in 1980/81 collection costs were £414 million as opposed to only £160 million disposal costs.   There is a conflict between reclamation and collection – larger, more powerful packer trucks make it harder to reclaim, but they are required for economic collection.   Local factors strongly influence the option whether to recycle separated fractions of MSW.   These factors can include, for example: a nearby papermill might favour the extraction of paper; a local shortage of natural gas could be offset by a gasification process; a local coal burning power station might benefit from refuse derived fuel substitution; chemical industry operations could use ethanol production by hydrolysis and fermentation or nearby metal smelting and glass industries could employ materials recovery as well as energy utilisation[6,120].

There are five basic methods for recovering values from raw refuse[20]:

- Incineration with direct energy conversion;
- Recovery of combustibles for direct use as fuel;

- Recovery of combustibles and conversion to fuel products - pyrolysis (solid fuel, oil, methane);

- Recovery of combustibles and separation into fuel and non-fuel products (paper for fibre or fuel, putrescibles for fuel or conversion to animal feed, plastics and other combustibles for fuel);

- Maximum recovery of all values (paper/plastic/organic for fuel or recycle, metals/glass for recycling) (Figure 86).

All of the options for MSW treatment eventually require some landfilling, in general operational costs and capital investments are inversely proportional to the land or volume consumed by the system. The density of landfill material converges to a common level after about six years, irrespective of the initial treatment used in its disposal. Incineration is the best option here, but the differences in density are much less than the theoretical differences in density between incinerated residue and compacted and covered refuse might suggest. The differences in space consumption by various systems are also rather less than the theoretical ratios might suggest[120].

Whilst there is a shortage of landfill resources close to urban areas, the mineral extraction industry in the United Kingdom is always creating more voids than there is waste to fill them with, and by and large there are adequate landfill spaces available for the foreseeable future. It is unlikely that landfill will not remain the predominant disposal system in the United Kingdom, but increasingly this will occur at more remote sites served by bulk transfer stations. This concentration of waste at one site provides excellent opportunities for recycling, although it should be remembered that landfill is inherently economic and attractive to Waste Disposal Authorities[120].

In most cases a waste reclamation plant will not pay its own way in conventional income and expenditure terms. Such plants are

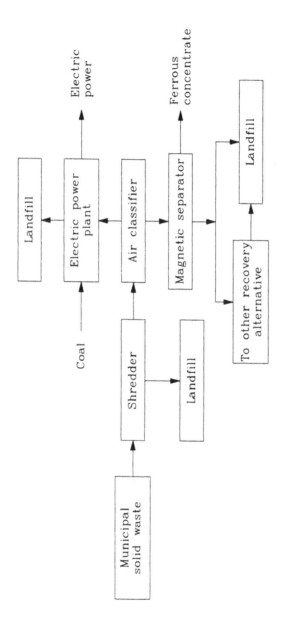

FIGURE 86. MSW processing flowsheet

designed to perform a waste disposal function and operate as reclamation units to economize on their operational costs.   In every case a contribution towards the treatment cost is called for by the waste-producing or disposing authority[121].

5.1 COMPOSITION OF URBAN WASTE

It is impossible to given an accurate composition of MSW.   The contents vary seasonally and long-term, and also with location (Figure 87)[24].   Composition ranges are more useful than averages, for instance Table 14 gives the range of compositions for samples from Washington DC in the period 1971-79[122].   Various sources quote values for the composition of MSW in the United Kingdom, one is given in Table 15[123].

TABLE 14.   MSW composition range, Washington DC, 1971-79.

Component	Composition wt%
Ferrous metals	4.4- 7.6
Aluminium	0.6- 1.1
Copper/zinc	0.1- 0.2
Glassy aggregates	4.2-16.5
Combustibles	62.8-83.0
Grit and dirt	2.0-13.9

5.2 MATERIAL RECOVERY

Any terminal waste treatment plant should be omnivorous, i.e. capable of receiving all consumer wastes, recovering as many materials as possible and converting the rest to inoffensive products with full energy utilization.   It should, however, be economically viable as a method of waste disposal - the most economically viable systems separate metals and refuse derived fuel (RDF), nothing else unless there is a local market for other reclaimed materials[6,24].

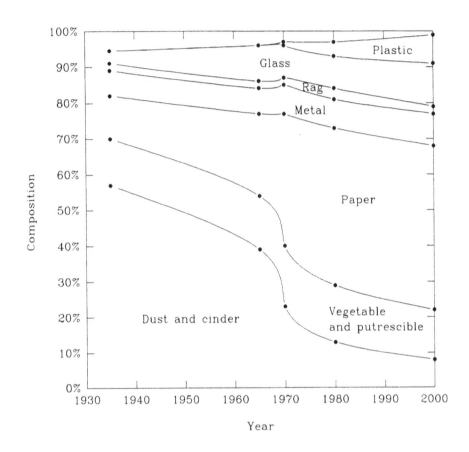

FIGURE 87.   Projected changes in the composition of domestic refuse in the United Kingdom

TABLE 15.   MSW composition, United Kingdom, 1983[123].

Component	Composition wt%
Metals	9.0
Glass	9.0
Vegetable and putrescible	21.0
Paper and board	30.0
Textiles	3.0
Plastics	3.0
Screenings	19.0
Unclassified	6.0

There are two distinct approaches to sorting and separating raw MSW. The first is the shred or pulp the waste to an approximately uniform size before classification, and the second is to sort by items into recyclable fractions. "Front-end" processes are material recovery operations performed on raw MSW before composting/incineration/pyrolysis, and "back-end" processes are the recovery of material after treatments such as composting, incineration and pyrolysis. Generally front-end operations only reduce the bulk of the weight by 15-20%, hence further processing is generally desirable.

Probably the most desirable system is one which recovers metals and glass, for construction, economically in a front end process and converts the combustible fraction to RDF as processing after the front end process becomes more difficult and expensive[6,12,19].

Recovery of a potentially valuable material from the solid waste stream is much more difficult than the recovery of homogeneous, uncontaminated manufacturing scrap. Mixing of the constituents in MSW renders some portions of the wastes practically unusable and salvaging these wastes therefore requires expenditures of power and labour in subsequent separation operations. The dominant characteristic of MSW is that it is heterogeneous.   The materials vary considerably in size, shape, and physical/chemical characteristics.   This creates difficulties as most of the separation equipment available has been developed for materials which are fairly homogeneous in physical characteristics so, in general, size reduction is desirable to obtain similar particle sizes[12].

Shredding is now commonly used to reduce the size of MSW before landfill, this also reduces problems due to rats and flies and fire risks are much lower.   Although shredders facilitate disposal of waste in landfilling by reducing volume and assisting compaction, their most important application is in resource recovery.   In general they are used to reduce waste to an average particle size of around 100 mm.   Shredders get heavy wear from constituents such as ball-bearings and glass and the energy requirements increase exponentially with increased reduction in size.

Reduction is expensive, the equivalent cost of shredding is less for high capacity systems, but it is advantageous whatever other treatment is used, if applied correctly.   For materials recovery, shredding is usually followed by overband magnetic separation and air classification to remove ferrous metals and light fibrous materials which would absorb water in subsequent wet processing such as water elutriation.   Hydropulping can be used to reduce organics to fine particles to be removed in a slurry while the dense particles sink and are recovered in good condition[6,19].

Dry screening can be very useful as a preconcentration step. Screening at 4.75 mm removes over 87% of dirt and glass in MSW, and only 4% of total combustibles - in many plants screening replaced previously installed air classifiers which tended to separate on the basis of overall aerodynamic properties, rather than density.   Dry screening may be difficult due to the water content of waste, this is not a problem in hydropulping systems where wet screening can be used.   Fine screenings from MSW processing are often useful as face cover for tips as they are usually inert[6,19,124].

Due to the heterogeneous nature of MSW, some problems are caused for air classification, it is not possible to separate small inorganics (e.g. glass) from large organics (e.g. orange peel). Research at Duke University Resource Recovery Laboratory in the United States produced an air classifier which separated on the basis of density alone and was not affected by particle shape/size. This separator used the principle that at the moment a particle starts its motion the velocity is zero, and therefore the drag is zero. Hence at t_o the drag force is no longer zero. A pulsed air flow should therefore lead to separation on the basis of density alone[124].

5.2.1 UNITED STATES BUREAU OF MINES PROCESSES

USBM has conducted extensive work on both a front and a back-end process. The front-end process uses dry separation techniques on raw refuse and it is typical of many processes; the back end process is for treating incinerator residue and is virtually unique. Only the front-end process will be discussed here.

Figure 88 gives the original USBM flowsheet and material balance. The products from this process are a ferrous concentrate, a combustibles concentrate (which can be used as fuel or further separated for paper recovery) and a non-combustible fraction (which can be discarded to landfill or further processed for glass recovery). The process was refined over several years to give the final flowsheet, Figure 89. This flowsheet produces a light gauge magnetic material suitable for commercial detinning, a massive non-ferrous concentrate, a massive ferrous concentrate, an aluminium concentrate, paper and plastic concentrates and glass cullet. The plant includes shredding, air classification, screening, gravity concentration and electrostatic separation[50,122].

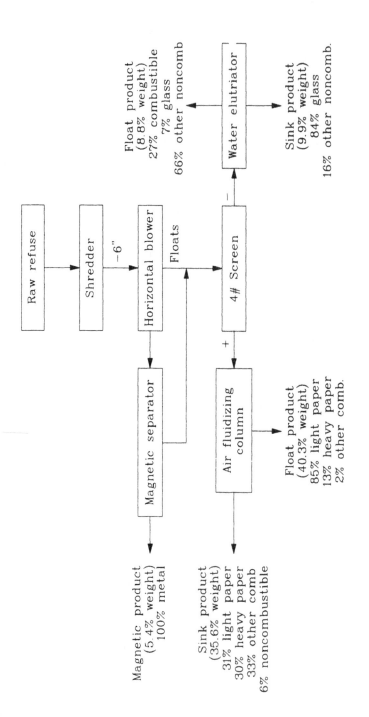

FIGURE 88. Flowsheet for reclamation of shredded raw refuse (USBM)

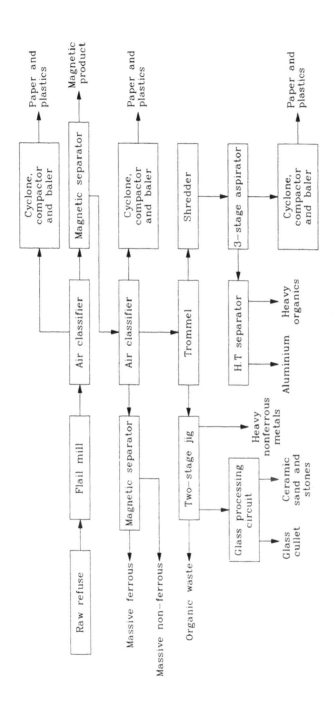

FIGURE 89. Raw refuse processing flowsheet (USBM)

For most of the research work the plant was tested at about 1-2 tons/hour although its rated capacity is 5 tons/hour.   The primary shredder is a double opposed flail mill, each rotor rated at 40 HP with variable speed.   Its function is to coarse shred the feed at low power to liberate materials in plastic and paper bags and cardboard boxes without damage and balling of metal objects. It was originally intended to use colour sorting of glass, so the flail mill was run at low speed (800 rpm) so that the glass particles were not reduced in size too much but when it was found to be uneconomic to colour sort the speed was increased to 1500 rpm to produce more closely sized materials for improved air classification.   The mill has no grates so that massive metals pass intact and are separated later.   Cans and other light gauge objects are dented or cut, but there is only minimum folding or balling in the flail mill[122,125,126].

The exhaust hood at the shredder discharge is used as a light air classifier with an air flow of 40 ft/s at the duct entrance. Only the lightest and cleanest paper and plastic is separated, it is recovered in cyclone 1, compacted, and then baled[122].

Once the very light paper and plastic has been removed, an overband magnetic separator is used to remove the light gauge ferrous metals.   These consist mainly of tin cans and are further shredded and sold for commercial detinning[122].

The non-magnetic reject is fed to an horizontal air classifier, with a chamber air speed of 42 ft/s.   The dry paper and plastic is carried to the far end of the air classifier, removed and recovered in cyclone 2.   It is then compacted and baled.   The very massive non-ferrous metals and the massive ferrous metals too heavy to be picked up by the primary magnetic separation stage fall closest to the feed end of the classifier. They are passed over a magnetic drum separator which separates the mixture into a massive non-ferrous concentrate, and a massive ferrous concentrate.   The massive metals are separated from the intermediate density products by a product splitter in the base of the chamber of the air classifier. This material consists of glass, non-ferrous metals, and heavy organics, with some paper and plastics[122].

The intermediate density material is transported by belt conveyor to a trommel. The trommel consists of a 4 ft diameter by 6 ft long screen. The screen has ¼" round holes, and rotates at 13 rpm. Undersize from the screen consists of glass and ceramics, a small amount of non-ferrous metals and 90% of the food and yard waste, and oversize includes aluminium and heavy organics, with paper and plastics[122].

The undersize from the trommel is transferred to a two-stage mineral jig via a belt conveyor with a magnetic head pulley which removes any remaining ferrous metals from the circuit. The heavy non-ferrous metals are removed from the waste as the sinks in the first stage of the jig, and the glass fraction of the waste makes up the sinks in the second stage of the jig. This glass aggregate contains up to 10% ceramics, stones, bones, aluminium, and other non-glass items. The light fraction from the second stage of the jig is dewatered on a vibratory screen - this fraction consists of organic wastes. The bottom grid of the jig in both stages removes fines that are minus $\frac{1}{8}$". These fines consist of some unrecovered glass, but mainly grit and dirt, and are sent to landfill[122].

The Bureau initially intended to clean the glass aggregate using optical sorting. In a primary optical sorter colourless glass and aluminium were to be separated from green and amber glass, which would be sorted in a secondary colour sorter into amber glass cullet and green glass cullet. The flint glass and aluminium would be passed through a rolls crusher and screened to obtain a flint glass and an aluminium concentrate. This process route, however, was found to be uneconomic, and a flotation circuit was designed to obtain a mixed colour glass cullet (Figure 90). The glass aggregate feed is impact crushed, and screened at

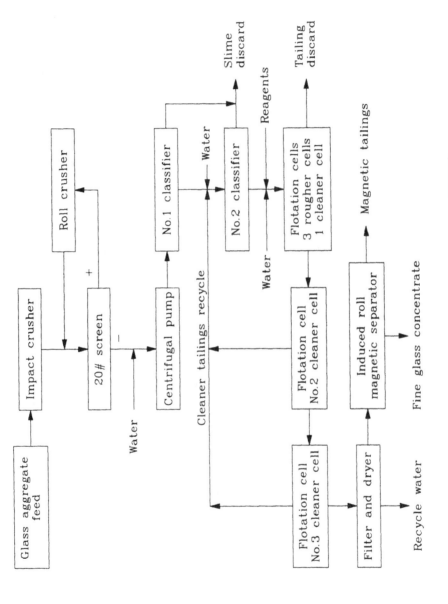

FIGURE 90. Continuous glass flotation process (USBM)

20 mesh. The plus 20 mesh is passed through a roll crusher and screened again. The minus 20 mesh is deslimed, and run through three rougher and three cleaner flotation cells, it is then filtered and dried and given a final cleaning by an induced roll magnetic separator to remove any magnetic impurities[21,122,125,127].

The plus ¼" trommel oversize is shredded in a 75 HP secondary knife-type shredder with a 2" grate opening. The product is treated in a three-stage aspirator. Shredded material is subjected to three air streams - one at the shredder grates, one at the opening in front of the aspirator, and one at the open bottom of the aspirator. This removes the remaining paper and light plastic which is recovered in cyclone 3 (Figure 89) and compacted and baled[122].

The heavies from the aspirator are dried and treated by a high tension separator which removes the heavy combustibles from the remaining metal (mainly aluminium)[122].

All of the air systems in this flowsheet are variable, each air classifier has a vari-speed exhaust blower, a baghouse filter and a cyclone collector. The operating cost of the plant (1976) was $8 per ton processed, the value of recovered products was $12.60 per ton and the fixed capital cost was $14.5 million[122].

USBM has also developed several flowsheets for the recovery of individual plastics from one another after recovery of mixed plastic waste from MSW. These mixed plastic wastes can be recovered from the plastic/paper air classifier products by electrostatic separation, recoveries of up to 99.4% plastic and 100% paper are attainable. One such process is given in Figure 91 where polyvinyl chloride, polystyrene, polyethylene and polypropylene are recovered. Another process developed by USBM recovers plastics, metal and fibre from Black Clawson concentrate (see below, and figure 92)[128,129,130].

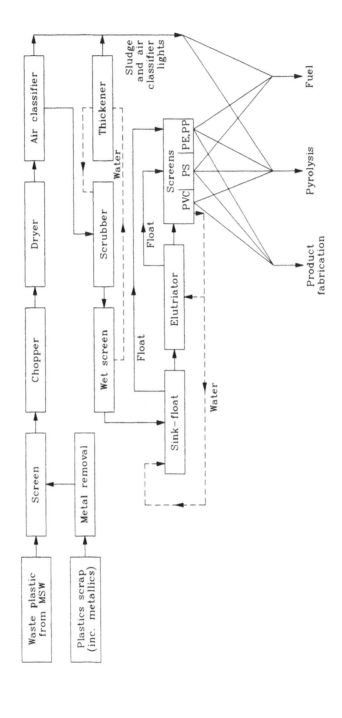

FIGURE 91. Plastics recovery flowsheet (USBM)

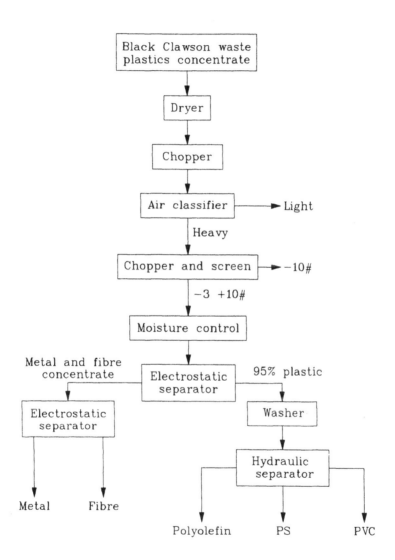

**FIGURE 92.   Plastics recovery from Black Clawson concentrate
(USBM)**

5.2.2 WARREN SPRING LABORATORY PROCESSES

Warren Spring Laboratory (WSL), Stevenage, England, developed its own circuit for treating raw, unburned refuse (Figure 93). The flowsheet uses a minimum of energy and capital expenditure to obtain as complete separation as possible. Refuse sack bursting, which lacerates sacks but does not comminute the contents, is followed by immediate trommel screening into four size fractions. This is to eliminate the need for primary shredding because although shredding provides some advantages in flow and liberation it can cause difficulties in subsequent cleaning operations. Shredding can cause dirt and grease to be spread over other constituents and it reduces paper's value as both a fuel and as secondary paper. Very fine glass produced in shredding can contaminate products, and tin cans can be distorted during shredding, leading to entrainment of impurities[19,121,131].

The trommel screens at 13, 50, and 200 mm. The plus 200 mm fraction (15 wt% of the feed) is air classified after fines removal, this reduces air cleaning requirements, and a paper rich product is retrieved. Pneumatic separations have advantages, but they are kept to a minimum on this flowsheet because the cost of air supply and cleaning can become prohibitive if used too extensively. The heavy particles from the air classifier are hammermilled and air classified again before being returned to the trommel[19,131].

The -200 mm +50 mm fraction (50 wt% of the feed) is carried under an overband magnetic separator, this size fraction contains virtually all of the tin cans. The magnetic concentrate is further processed to obtain a clean tin plate and a massive iron concentrate. Non-magnetics are transported away on a high speed conveyor which is used as a ballistic separator. A rotating drum is used as a self cleaning splitter and a gentle air blower supplements the separating action (Figure 35). This separates a light organic fraction from a dense fraction containing glass

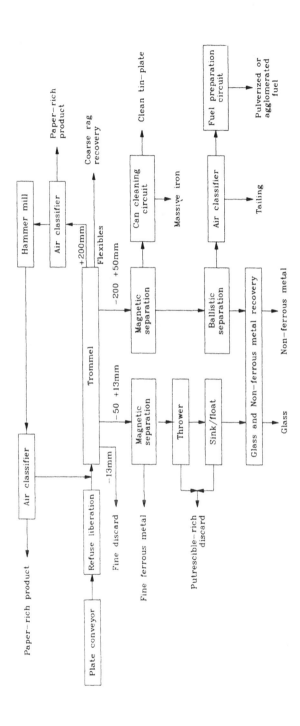

FIGURE 93. Raw refuse processing flowsheet (WSL)

bottles, stones, large bones, non-ferrous metal objects (such as cooking utensils), books and catalogues, etc. This dense fraction can be treated by a combination of selective comminution, air classification, and froth flotation to obtain non-ferrous metal and glass concentrates. A low grade fuel product can be obtained from the ballistic separator lights by processing in a rotary drum air classifier[19,131].

The -50 mm +13 mm fraction (20 wt% of the feed) is magnetically separated to remove fine ferrous metal. Non-magnetic rejects are passed to a WSL thrower/separator which relies on a combination of aerodynamic, impact and sliding friction effects to separate a low density product made up mainly of small pieces of paper, vegetable and garden wastes and low density plastic, and a high density product containing dense vegetable matter, broken glass, bones, dense plastics, and metallic objects. The high density product is treated by HMS at s.g 1.15 in brine. At this density all of the vegetable matter floats and the glass, pottery and metallics sink. This sink product can be treated by selective comminution to obtain a mixed non-ferrous metal concentrate and a mixed glass concentrate[19,131].

The -13 mm fraction represents about 15% of the feed and is made up mainly of dust, dirt, ashes, grit, and fine cinders, with insignificant quantities of paper, metals and glass, and can be discarded. The plant recovers a fine ferrous concentrate, a massive iron concentrate, a clean tin plate fraction, a non-ferrous metals concentrate and a glass concentrate. There are also several combustible products obtained which could be used for material recycling or as a low grade fuel[19,121,131].

The Doncaster Project. A municipal waste reclamation plant, based on the WSL flowsheet, was built in 1977 at Kirk Sandall in Doncaster, England (Figure 94). It was a joint venture between the waste disposal authority (South Yorkshire County Council) and

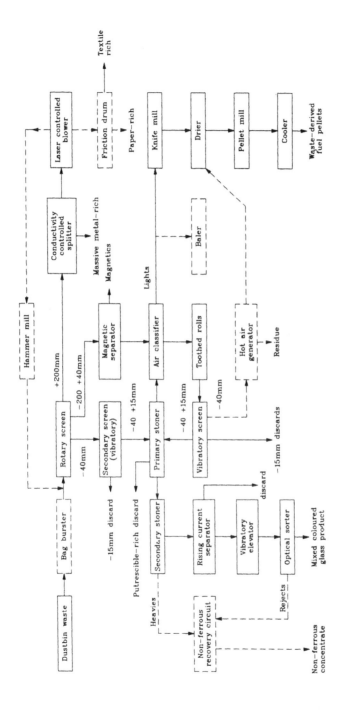

FIGURE 94. Doncaster refuse processing plant

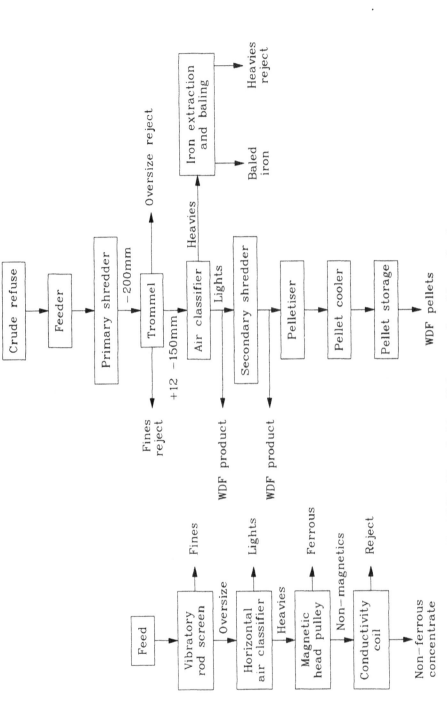

FIGURES 95 and 96. Byker reclamation plant

the United Kingdom Department of the Environment. There were several reasons for its construction - there was a shortage of suitable landfill sites near to hand, it was a serious effort to reclaim useful materials from refuse, and it was hoped to reduce the operating costs of waste disposal with the sale of reclaimed materials. The whole plant was built under cover, at a capital cost of £2 227 000, to process 10-20 tons/hour[3,121].

The Byker Reclamation Plant. Another United Kingdom Department of the Environment venture, this time in association with Tyne and Wear County Council, is at Byker, Newcastle-Upon-Tyne (Figure 95). Again this plant is based on the WSL flowsheet, but it is much simpler, the only products being waste derived fuel (WDF) and baled iron[24,121].

Both the Doncaster and Byker plants operated successfully, although the Doncaster plant has now been closed. WSL have conducted more work on the Byker circuit to enable recovery of non-ferrous metals from the pulverized refuse. The majority of the non-ferrous metals (85 wt%) are contained in the heavy fraction, but they are diluted with fines (56% -10 mm) and combustibles (30.9%) and so a non-ferrous recovery flowsheet was developed (Figure 96)[121,132].

5.2.3 MUNICIPAL REFUSE RECYCLING PLANTS IN THE UNITED STATES

New Orleans, Louisiana. The National Center for Resource Recovery (NCRR - Washington DC) 500 ton/day flowsheet is shown in Figure 97. The idea is to use it as a front end system which can discharge to an incinerator or a composter already in the vicinity (80% of the feed by weight). A plant adapted from this flowsheet has been built in New Orleans (Figure 98). The basis behind the plant agrees with the WSL logic - that trommel screening before comminution is desirable. The plant has a capacity of 650 tons/day, and includes two primary shredders. Both of the

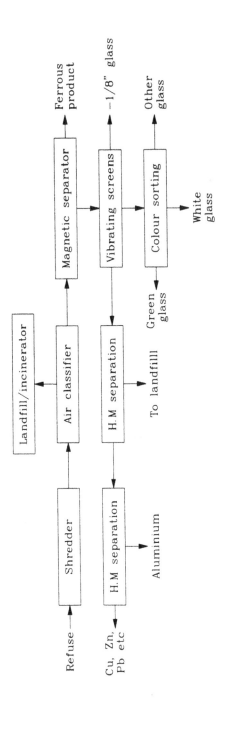

FIGURE 97. NCCR "front end" system

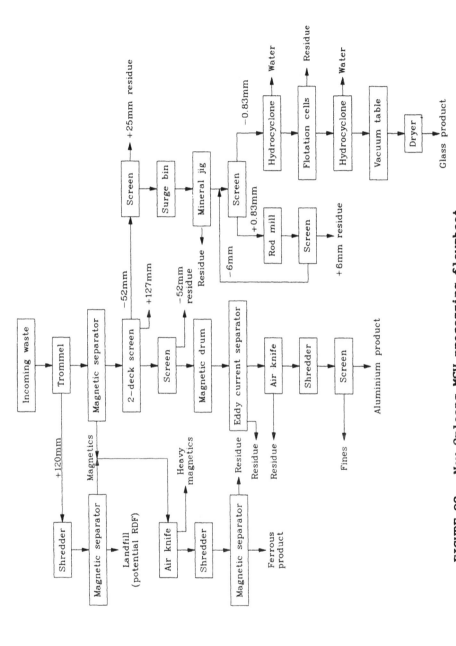

FIGURE 98. New Orleans MSW processing flowsheet

shredders have a capacity of 62.5 tons/hour - shredder 1 is preceded by a 4" trommel, and shredder 2 has no trommel as it is used for back-up and oversize material[12,29,133,134].

The ferrous recovery system consists of magnetic drum separators, the magnetics are then air classified in a ferrous metal classifier to give a light fraction, a light ferrous fraction and a heavy ferrous fraction. The non-magnetics are air classified and the heavies go to the aluminium recovery system. This consists of a two-deck screen which produces a +4" fraction (to landfill); a -4" +2" fraction which is passed over a drum magnet and on to a linear induction motor eddy current separator (gives an aluminium product, a non-ferrous metal product and an organic product); and a -2" product which goes to the glass recovery circuit. This -2" product is screened at 1" (the oversize is discarded) and the undersize is jigged. The products from the jig are a light organic fraction, a glass rich fraction and a non-ferrous fraction. The glass rich fraction is screened at 20 mesh and the oversize is rod milled and screened at ¼". The undersize is returned to the 20 mesh screen. Desliming of the -20 mesh fraction occurs in a hydrocyclone, and it is then treated in a froth flotation circuit to obtain a glass product[134].

Monroe County, New York, Resource Recovery Facility. This plant, for recovery of 2000 tonnes/day, is shown in detail in Figure 99. More than 50% of the output is as RDF to be sold for burning in coal fired suspension boilers. The plant is designed to produce the highest quality recovered materials from the waste stream consistent with the available markets for the sale of such materials, and dependent on the availability of a reliable technology for producing the desired material. For example, the plant produces a light and heavy ferrous product, rather than a single mixed product, and it also produces a clean mixed colour glass cullet for remelting. Ninety to 95% of the incoming waste is recovered, the energy recovered in the RDF is ten times the

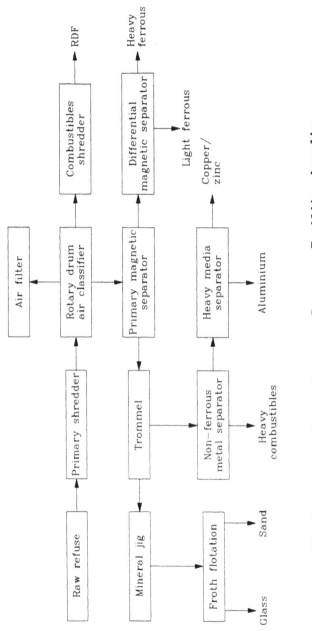

FIGURE 99. Monroe County Resource Recovery Facility, baseline process

energy   required   to   power   the   resource   recovery
facility[135,136,137].

A baseline process, consisting of two identical process
lines, employs a coarse preliminary shredding and an air
classification step which separates the stream into light and
heavy fractions. The two primary shredders are 1000 HP, 70
tonne/hour units which run at 720 RPM with reversible motors. The
product from the shredders (-300 mm) is treated by four 35
tonne/hour rotary drum air classifiers which are 2.75 m diameter
by 8.5 m long[135,137].

The light fraction (RDF) is screened, glass dirt and grit
makes up the undersize, and the oversize goes to a secondary
shredder which is a 932 kW reversible hammermill. Material
consisting of paper, film plastic and light combustibles is
reduced in size to 90% -19 mm, and is transferred via pneumatic
conveyor to a compactor[135].

The heavy fraction from the air classifiers is magnetically
separated (34 tonnes/hour) and 95% of the ferrous metal is removed
to be processed in the ferrous refining module. The heavy
non-ferrous material is screened in a 2.75 m diameter trommel with
19 mm holes. The undersize is glass rich. The trommel oversize
consists of heavy combustibles, putrescibles and non-ferrous
metals, and it is reshredded in a horizontal, 597 kW hammermill to
50 mm. The shredder product is treated in a zigzag air classifier
- the lights go to make RDF and the heavies go to another stage of
magnetic separation and to an eddy current separator to remove the
non-ferrous metal from the heavy combustibles[135].

In the ferrous refining module a differential magnetic
separator is used to further classify the scrap as a light or
heavy fraction. The light ferrous fraction is reshredded to be
sold to the de-tinning market[135].

The non-ferrous product from the eddy current separator is
treated in a Wemco HMS system at s.g 3.0 in the non-ferrous

refining module. The trommel undersize is treated in the residue recovery module. A mineral jig removes the light organics for landfill and the glassy aggregate is comminuted in a rod mill. The product from the rod mill is screened to give an oversize metallic concentrate, to be processed in the non-ferrous recovery module, and a glass rich undersize. A desliming classifier is used before primary flotation of the glass rich undersize. The product from this goes to a spiral classifier and secondary flotation, which is followed by wet magnetic separation, during which the glass is upgraded by the removal of sand, ceramics, ferrous particles and other impurities. Clean sand is recovered by the primary flotation. The glass fraction is filtered by a dewatering sand filter and then dried in a rotary drier to give a high purity mixed colour glass product, with less than 1% moisture[135].

The outputs from the system are RDF (66.3%), heavy combustibles (4.7%), mixed glass cullet (8.7%), light ferrous (6.6%), heavy ferrous (0.3%), aluminium (0.35%), heavy non-ferrous (0.05%), sand (3.2%) and light waste for landfill (8.8%). This plant was not expected to make a profit but to approach the cost of landfilling. Unfortunately, resource recovery can only succeed when local circumstances are ripe for it, and this was confirmed by the Monroe County facility which suffered great difficulties[135,138].

City of Ames, Iowa, Resource Recovery System. The Ames Resource Recovery System is a completely dry separation system which recovers metals and a solid fuel type product (RDF). The plant was designed to process 186 tons/day (Figure 100). Two-stage shredding is followed by magnetic separation, air density separation, and non-ferrous separation to produce a ferrous concentrate, an aluminium concentrate, a non-ferrous concentrate and RDF, which is stored and then fired as a coal supplement in the city power plant. With an annual feed of 48 000 tons of solid

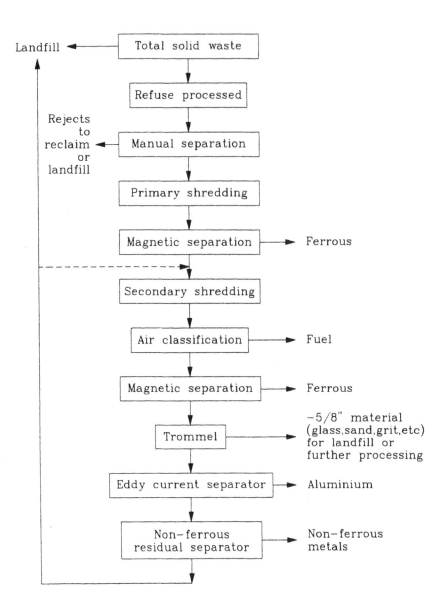

FIGURE 100.   Ames Resource Recovery System

waste, 3000 tons of ferrous metal can be reclaimed and sold, and 84% can be converted to fuel with a value of 19.3 M kWh (electrical energy generated) - with the consumption of only 2.8 M kWh[24,139,140].

Miami, Florida, Resource Recovery Plant. The Miami Resource Recovery Plant is designed to process 3000 tonnes/day, on a three-shift, seven days-a-week basis. It generates and sells electricity, sells ferrous and non-ferrous metals, and glass, and breaks even on revenue to operating cost. Each week 700-1000 tonnes of ferrous scrap is sold. The total capital cost for the plant, which employs 200 operating staff and 25 administration staff, was $150 million. The feed consists of household garbage and trash (garden wastes, white goods, furniture, etc.) from around Dade County - the county pays 43 cents per tonne for this disposal service. A typical waste profile for Dade County is 55% combustibles, 25% water, 8% glass, 7% ferrous metals, 1% aluminium and 4% miscellaneous non-combustibles. From this waste the plant recovers, per year, 62 000 tonnes ferrous metals, 20-85 000 tonnes glass, 10 000 tonnes miscellaneous non-ferrous metals, 3000 tonnes aluminium, and generates 450-600 000 Megawatt hours of electricity[141].

Household garbage treatment - bags of garbage are ripped open and trommel screened at 2½". The undersize consists mainly of broken glass, the oversize contains cans, paper, plastic, rubber, wood, etc. One hydropulper is used to comminute the undersize, and three are used for the oversize. Each hydropulper is 20 ft in diameter and fed by continuously recycled well water. A rotating tackle creates a whirling slurry of contents and the centrifugal force brings the heavy materials (primarily metallics) to the periphery for removal by bucket elevators. These materials are magnetically separated to give clean steel and non-ferrous metal, which is treated in a mineral reclamation plant. The slurry is pumped to centrifugal cleaners which eject small and heavy particles.   The slurry is about 4-5% solids and is dewatered to 50% solids in a dewatering press (two-stage).   This RDF (mainly organics - paper, plastic, wood) is taken to the boiler house. The electricity generated is enough for 50-60 000 of the areas homes.   The boiler ash is sold to cement manufacturers or used as landfill cover[141].   Trash treatment - The trash is initially treated in a dry process.   It is passed through a size reduction stage, magnetically separated and then screened at 1-2¼".   The oversize is treated in the hydropulpers and the undersize is air classified.   The lights from the air separation are used as fuel for the boilers, and the heavies consist of metals, stones and ceramics which are separated in the mineral reclamation plant. The glass is sold for construction and the recovered non-ferrous metals - aluminium, brass, bronze, copper, lead, zinc and electrical motors are sold to local scrap dealers.   Approximately 20 tonnes/day, less than 1% of the input, is sent to landfill[141].

Akron, Ohio, Recycle Energy System (RES).   The Akron RES treats 750-1000 tons/day with a simple process.   The facility shreds waste to a nominal 6" size and passes it over two magnetic drum separators.   The recovered ferrous fraction is cleaned by an air scrubbing system - about 9000 tons/year of ferrous metal is sold. The rest of the waste is used to produce around 400 000 lbs of steam/hour[142].

Franklin, Ohio, Black Clawson Process.   This is another plant to use hydropulping which has the advantage of giving a cleaner product, but creates the disadvantage of having waste water disposal (Figure 101).   The raw refuse is treated in a hydropulper, the dense metals are recovered from the outside of the hydropulper and magnetically separated.   A ferrous concentrate is obtained using an overband magnetic separator and the non-magnetics are treated in the glass and aluminium recovery sub-circuit.   The slurry from the hydropulper is passed through a hydrocyclone, the flow under is also treated in the glass and

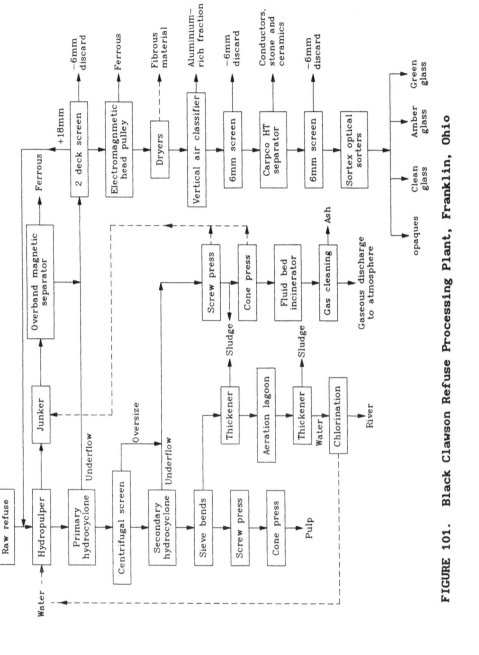

FIGURE 101. Black Clawson Refuse Processing Plant, Franklin, Ohio

aluminium sub-circuit. The dense materials to the glass and aluminium recovery sub-circuit are screened on a double-deck vibratory screen. The -6 mm fraction is discarded and the +18 mm fraction is returned to the hydropulper. The -18 mm +6 mm fraction is magnetically separated over an electromagnetic head pulley to obtain a ferrous concentrate and the non-magnetics are then dried, and fibrous materials are recovered. A vertical air classifier is used to obtain an aluminium-rich fraction. The lighter fraction from the air classifier is electrostatically treated to remove any conductors and then the glass-rich material is treated by electronic colour sorting to obtain flint, green and amber glass[24].

La Verne, California, Garret Process. The Garret Research and Development Company, and Occidental Research Corporation, developed a front-end resource recovery system to the Garret flash pyrolysis system (Figure 102). Primary shredding reduces the waste to a -4" product which is magnetically separated and then air classified to give 65% of the feed material in the overflow of the air classifier (this contains 30% of the glass, 20% of the aluminium and 75% of the organics). The overflow is dried and screened - the oversize forming most of the feed to the flash pyrolysis unit (after secondary shredding). The undersize (-8 mesh) is treated on an air table to obtain a glass preconcentrate which is cleaned up by froth flotation. The underflow from the air classifier is trommel screened - the undersize goes to the froth flotation section and the oversize is treated on a linear induction motor eddy current separator to recover an aluminium concentrate[19,143].

Hempstead, New York, Process. The first full-scale commercial application of an optical sorting system was built at Hempstead, New York. The plant recovers ferrous metals, a mixed non-ferrous product (by use of HMS and jigging), an aluminium concentrate (from an electrostatic separator) and flint, green and amber glass

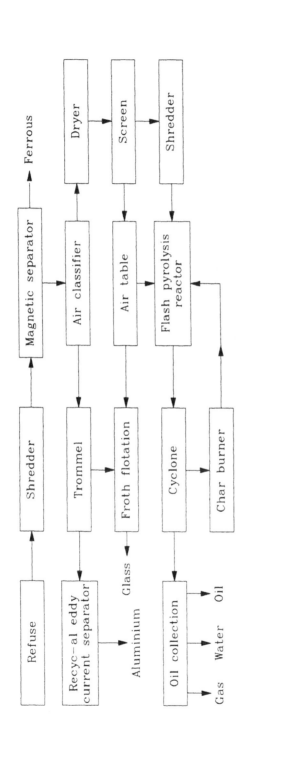

FIGURE 102. Garret Process, Occidental Research Corporation, California

products (Figure 103)[39].

5.2.4 OTHER PROCESSES

Massachusetts Institute of Technology.   MIT has devised an automated item identification flowsheet (Figure 104). Loose paper and plastic film are removed in an air stream.   Undersize is removed for shredding and air classification in the conventional way, the oversize is discharged into carts on an oval track. Metal detection, impact sensing and infra-red sensing is analysed by computer and the cart is dumped into various stations.   If no conclusive relationship is reached, the large item is returned for shredding with the undersize. The system identifies glass, metal, plastic and cellulose with a greater than 90% accuracy[6].

Plastic Recycling.   With the recent public concern with environmental issues, the economics of plastic recycling has improved considerably, and several plastic recycling plants have opened - some of the larger consumer product corporations use the fact that their packaging is made up partly of recycled plastic as a selling point. Reprise opened a bottle recycling pilot plant in Blackpool England, to separate bottles made of different plastics - PVC, PET and polyolefins. The plant uses x-rays to activate the chlorine in PVC which gives a distinct emission spectrum which is electronically detected. Air blasts sort the PVC bottles from the rest of the mixed stream. The remaining mixture consists of PET and polyolefins which are separated on the basis of specific gravity. Approximately 20 000 bottles (1 tonne) are treated each hour[144].

5.3 SUMMARY

The recovery of materials from solid waste is not easy to achieve in an economic context. Many of the systems illustrated above have not been completely successful, this has usually been due to the wrong plants being utilised at the wrong locations at the

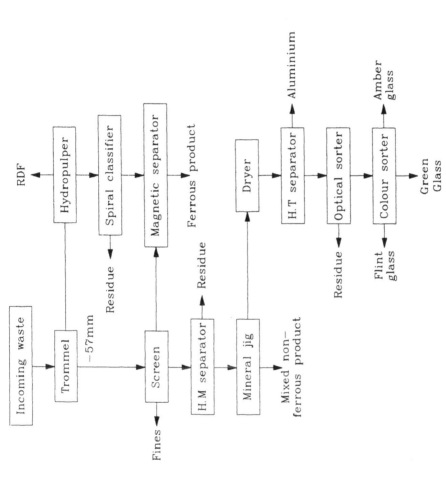

FIGURE 103. Refuse processing plant, Hempstead, New York

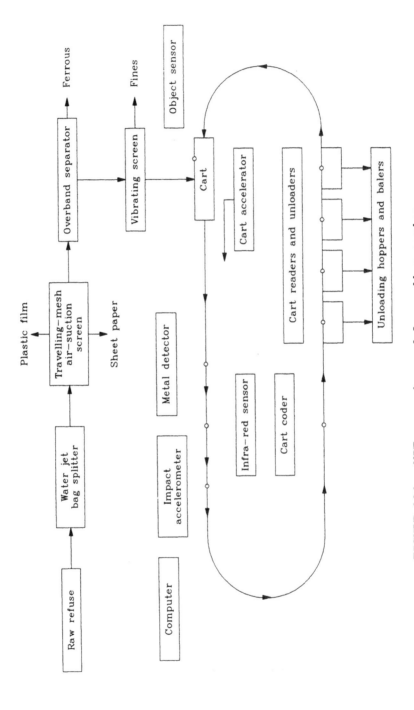

FIGURE 104. MIT presorter and large item sorter

wrong time. Others, however, have achieved limited success as waste disposal alternatives. The potential for improved success in the recovery of materials from MSW has increased considerably with the introduction of low capital and running cost eddy current separators. These can effectively separate the non-ferrous metals from waste with the minimum of processing, this development coupled with the high intrinsic value of non-ferrous metals could lead to a greater number of recycling plants being developed, despite the reservations due to some of the poor results obtained in the past.

The development of eddy current separators could also lead to an increase in the viability of source separation, the biggest problem in source separation is the efficiency of collection. Some source separation schemes operate vehicles with separate compartments for each material. This leads to some compartments being filled while others are left empty but now it is probably justified to have a two compartment vehicle in which the paper is collected separately from everything else. The components of the other compartment could be passed over an eddy current separator at a central site, recovering a ferrous and a non-ferrous concentrate, and a waste fraction.

REFERENCES

1. H. Spoel (1990). The current status of scrap metal recycling. *Journal of Metals*, pp. 38-41.

2. The Institution of Metallurgists (1977). Reclamation and recycling of metals. Autumn Review Course, series 3, no. 8.

3. C. Thomas (1979). *Material gains*. Earth Resources Research Ltd. London.

4. United Kingdom Secretary of State for the Environment and Secretary of State for Industry (1974). *War on Waste - A Policy for Reclamation*. Government Green Paper. HMSO.

5. Waste Management Advisory Council (1976). First report of the Waste Management Advisory Council. HMSO.

6. A. Barton (1976). *Recycling*. School of Mathematics and Physical Sciences, Murdoch University, Western Australia.

7. M. Sittig, ed. Metal and inorganic waste reclaiming encyclopedia. Noyes Data Corporation, New Jersey. *Pollution Technology Review no. 70*. Chemical Technology Review no. 175.

8. Environmental Resources Ltd. (for the Environment and Consumer Protection Service of the Commission of the European Communities) (1976). *The Economics of Recycling*. Graham and Trotman Ltd.

9. M. J. Spendlove (1977). Bureau of Mines Research on Resource Recovery - reclamation, disposal and stabilisation. USBM, IC 8750.

10. K. J. Thomé-Kozmiensky, ed. (1979). Recycling Berlin '79. E. Freitung-Verlag für Umwelttechnik, Berlin, 2 vol.

11. Lord Avebury (1973). *New Scientist*. 22 Feb.

12. J.L. Pavoni, J.E. Heer Jr, and D.J. Hagerty (1975). *Handbook of Solid Waste Disposal - Materials and Energy Recovery*. Van Nostrand Reinhold Co. New York.

13. S.A. Bortz, K.B. Higbie (1980). *Materials Recycling - an Overview of the Sixth Mineral Waste Utilisation Symposium*. USBM, IC 8826.

14. W.U. Chandler (1986). Materials recycling: the virtue of necessity. *Conservation and recycling*, vol. 9. no. 1, pp. 87-109.

15. R.F. Testin (1981). Aluminium recycling - potential and problems. *Journal of Metals*, pp. 21-24.

16. M.E. Henstock (1988). *Design for Recyclability*. Institute of Metals.

17. Meadows, *et al* (1972). *Limits to Growth*. Pan Books.

18. M.E. Henstock. The need for materials recycling (see Ref. 2).

19. A. Porteus (1977). *Recycling Resources Refuse*. Longman, New York.

20. M.J. Spendlove (1976). *Recycling trends in the United States: a review*. USBM, IC 8711.

21. M.E. Henstock, ed. (1983). *Disposal and Recovery of Municipal solid Waste*. Butterworth and Co. London.

22. P.M. Sullivan, M.H. Stanczyk and M.J. Spendlove (1973). *Resource Recovery from Raw Urban Refuse*. USBM, RI 7760.

23. United Kingdom Department of the Environment (1976). *Reclamation Treatment and Disposal of Wastes - an Evaluation of Available Options* (1976). HMSO Waste Management Paper No. 1.

24. A.V. Bridgwater, and C.J. Mumford (1979). *Waste Recycling and Pollution Control Handbook*. George Godwin Ltd. London.

25. T.J. Veasey (1990). *Reclamation*. School of Chemical Engineering, University of Birmingham. Course ChE 344 (Mineral Processing).

26. Departments of Minerals Engineering and Extramural Studies,

University of Birmingham and the Minerals Engineering Society (1975). *The Technology of Reclamation Symposium.* University of Birmingham. Apr. 7-11.

27. C.B. Kanahan, *et al* (1973). *Bureau of Mines Research Programs on Recycling and Disposal of Mineral-, Metal- and Energy-based Wastes.* USBM, IC 8595.

28. D.P. Monaghan (1990). Ferrous Scrap Metal Reclamation and the Recycling Industry - its Value to the Economy and the Environment. *Recycling of Metalliferrous Materials.* Institution of Mining and Metallurgy, Birmingham, England. April 23-25.

29. D.F. Anderson (1987). Scrap as a commodity. *Ironmaking and Steelmaking.* Vol 14, no. 3, pp. 130-135.

30. K.J. Thomé-Kozmiensky. *Energy and Material Recycling* (see Ref. 10, vol. 1).

31. D. Pearson and M. Webb (1973). The salvage and recycling of useful materials. *The Chemical Engineer.* Feb.

32. General Electric Co. (1975). *Solid Waste Management - Technology Assessment.* Van Nostrand Reinhold Co., New York.

33. J.W. Sawyer (1974). *Automotive Scrap Recycling - Processes, Prices and Prospects.* Resources for the Future, Inc.

34. M.C. Munson (1990). USBM Surveys Mineral and Metal Commodities. *Journal of Metals.* pp. 49-51.

35. M.B. Bever (1978). Systems aspects of materials recycling. *Conservation and recycling.* Vol. 2, pp. 1-17.

36. D.G. Wilson (1977). History of Solid Waste Management. *Handbook of Solid Waste Management.* D.G. Wilson, ed. Van Nostrand Reinhold Co., New York.

37. Theodor Koller (1918). The utilization of waste products - a treatise on the rational utilization. *Recovery and Treatment of Waste products of All Kinds.* Scott, Greenwood and Son, London.

38. P.A. Vesilind and A.E. Rimer (1981). *Unit Operations in*

Resource Recovery Engineering. Prentice Hall Inc., New Jersey.

39. J. Campbell and S. Russell (1983). Resource recovery; technology. *Conservation and Recycling*. Vol. 6, no. 4, pp. 147-149.

40. R. New, R. Papworth and M. Webb (1963). *Sizing Fragmentizer Residues Using a Vibrating Rod Grizzly*. Warren Spring Laboratory, LR 452 (MR).

41. Newell Industries Inc. (1991). *Literature Produced for the Institute of Scrap Recycling Industries National Convention*. Las Vegas, Nevada.

42. Lindemann KG. *Kondirator*. Lindemann pamphlet.

43. K.C. Dean, *et al* (1983). *Bureau of Mines Research on Recycling Scrap Automobiles*. USBM, Bulletin 684.

44. Lindemann KG. *Zerdirator*. Lindemann pamphlet.

45. N.A. Rowson, F.A. Garner and T.J. Veasey (1990). Thermally assisted liberation of copper from copper/plastic scrap. *Recycling of Metalliferous Materials*. Institution of Mining and Metallurgy. Birmingham, England. Apr. 23-25.

46. C. Eddolls (1990). Coopers Metals Ltd., Swindon, UK, private communication.

47. F.L. Stirrup (1965). *Public Cleaning, Refuse Disposal*. Pergamon Press, Oxford.

48. L.J. Froisland, *et al* (1975). *Recovering Metal from Non-magnetic Autoshredder Reject*. USBM, RI 8049.

49. B.A. Wills (1988). *Mineral Processing Technology*. 4th edn., Pergamon Press, Oxford.

50. K.S. Dean, C.J. Chindaran and L. Peterson (1971). *Preliminary Separation of Metals and Non-metals from Urban Refuse*. USBM, TPR 34.

51. R. Papworth (1980). *Development of a Horizontal Air Classifier to Concentrate Non-ferrous Metals from Sized Fragmentizer Residues*. Warren Spring Laboratory, LR 538

(MR)M.

52. Anon (1982). New Bulldog System Aids Metal Recovery. *Recycling Today*. January, p. 132.

53. S. Khalafalla and G.W. Reimers (1981). *Beneficiation with Magnetic Fluids*. USBM, RI 8532.

54. J. Shimoiizaka, *et al* (1980). Sing-float separators using permanent magnets and water-based magnetic fluid. *IEEE Transactions on Magnetics*. Vol. mag-16, no. 2. pp. 368-371.

55. M.E. Henstock, ed. (1974). *The recycling and disposal of solid Waste*. Proceedings of a course organised by the Department of Metallurgy and Materials Science, University of Nottingham. Apr. 1-5.

56. Newell Engineering Ltd. *Aluminium Can Separators*. Newell Data Sheet, no. 83/89.

57. C.P. Manufacturing Ltd. *CanPak OC1207 Can Sorter*. Portable Balers Ltd. pamphlet.

58. J. Pearce, D. Engledow (1987). Developments of scrap beneficiation by British Steel Corporation. *Ironmaking and Steelmaking*. Vol. 14, no. 5, pp. 246-252.

59. J.L. Holman, J.B. Stephenson and M.J. Adam (1974). *Recycling of Plastics from Urban and Industrial Refuse*. USBM, RI 7955.

60. Cotswold Research Ltd. *Cotswold Separator*. Bird Group of Companies pamphlet.

61. Eriez Magnetics UK Ltd. *Non-ferrous Eddy Current Separators*. Eriez Magnetics pamphlet.

62. Newell Engineering Ltd. (1990). *Newell Announce the Launch of their New Permanent Magnetic Non-ferrous Separator*. Newell information sheet. Wastemann '90 Exhibition.

63. Outokumpu Electronics Division. *Precon - Ore Preconcentrator*. Outokumpo Electronics Division pamphlet.

64. Outokumpu Electronics Division. *Rapid Metal Sorting and Analysis by X-ray Fluorescence*. Clandon Scientific Ltd. pamphlet.

65. R.D. Brown, Jr., W.D. Riley and D.M. Soboroff (1986). Sorting techniques for mixed metal scrap. *Conservation and Recycling.* Vol. 9, no. 1, pp. 73-86.

66. W.R. Hibbard, Jr. (1982). The extractive metallurgy of old scrap recycle. *Journal of Metals.* July, pp. 50-53.

67. W.L. Dalmijn, W.P.H. Voskuyl and H.J. Roorda (1978). *Recovery of aluminium alloys from shredded automobiles.* Complex Metallurgy '78. Institution of Mining and Metallurgy, pp. 75-81.

68. E.A. Kinne (1980). *Options for the Collection and Recovery of Household Appliance Materials.* See ref. 13.

69. M.E. Henstock (1979). *Resource Recovery from Automobiles.* See ref. 10, vol. 2.

70. R. Weber (1979). *For Recycling of Some Non-iron Metals of Autombile Wrecks.* See ref. 10, vol. 2.

71. D.A. Harrison, P.C. Newdick and P.J. Bowles (1974). Recovery of non-ferrous metals from car scrap. *Metals and Materials.* Jan., pp. 59-65.

72. E. Scalcemann (1980). *Separation of Non-ferrous Metals in Automobile Scrap by Means of Permanent Magnets.* See ref. 13.

73. M. Wutz (1979). *Recycling - Technologies and Cycling of Materials in the Field of Motor Vehicles.* See ref. 10, vol. 2.

74. M. Adolph (1979). *Recycling of Raw Materials from the Disused Motor Car.* See ref. 10, vol. 2.

75. K.C. Dean and J.W. Sterner (1969). *Dismantling a Typical Junk Automobile to Produce Quality Scrap.* USBM, RI 7350.

76. J.W. Sterner, D.K. Steele and M.B. Shirts (1984). *Hand Dismantling and Shredding of Japanese Automobiles to Determine Material Contents and Metal Recoveries.* USBM, RI 8855.

77. P. Cordes (1983). If you know Venti Oelde you also know the best system. *Recycling Today,* Apr.

78. R.D.R. McChesney (1979). *Recovering Shredded Non-ferrous Metals with Water and Heavy Media Separation Systems*. See ref. 10, vol. 2.

79. Airtechnik Venti Oelde. *Advanced Air Handling Technology*. Ventilatorenfabrik Oelde GmbH pamphlet.

80. M. Rousseau and A. Melin (1990). Reclamation of non-ferrous metals from shredded scrap. *Recycling of Metalliferrous Materials*. Institution of Mining and Metallurgy, Birmingham, England. Apr. 23-25.

81. L.J. Froisland, K.C. Dean and C.J. Chindgren (1972). *Upgrading Junk Autoshredder Rejects*. USBM, TPR 53.

82. C.J. Chindgren, K.C. Dean and LeRoy Peterson (1971). *Recovery of the Non-ferrous Metals from Autoshredder Rejects by Air Classification*. USBM, TPR 31.

83. Joseph W. Sterner (1982). A water elutriator system for recovery of non-ferrous metals. *Scrap Age*. April. pp. 168-171.

84. D.K. Steele and J.W. Sterner (1983). *A Water Elutriator System for Recovering Non-magnetic Metals from Autoshredder Rejects*. USBM, RI 6771.

85. Newell Engineering Ltd. *Newell Wet Shredding System*. Advertisement sheet.

86. Anon. (1983). Venti Oelde: New fragmentizer-sized heavy media system. *Recycling Today*. Aug.

87. S. Ghosh, M. Coxon and P. Schmidt (1988). Vibratory sorting of shredder scrap. *Aufbereitungs-Technik*. No. 1, pp. 22-25.

88. A.T. Basten and H.H. Dreisen (1977), assigned to Stamicarbon BV, Netherlands. US Patent 4 036 441. July 19.

89. Anon. (1981). Heavy media plant taps secondary metal resource. *Engineering and Mining Journal*. June, pp. 51-53.

90. R.J. Wilson (1991). *Scrap Metal Processing*. School of Chemical Engineering, University of Birmingham, course ChE 344 (Mineral Processing).

91. Le Comptoir Industriel des Metaux et Plastiques. *CIMP Resources Recovery Systems*. CIMP (UK) Ltd. pamphlet.

92. Anon. (1975). Cryogenic scrap fragmentizing. *Energy Digest*. Dec.

93. K. Harrison, S.G. Tong and N.C. Hilyard (1986). An economic evaluation of cryogenic grinding of automotive tyres. *Conservation and Recycling*. Vol. 9, no. 1, pp. 1-14.

94. B.W. Dunning, Jr. (1980). *Characterisation of Scrap Electronic Equipment for Resource Recovery*. See ref. 13.

95. P.A. Neenan (1990). Challenges and opportunities in steel can recycling. *Recycling of Metalliferrous Materials*. Institution of Mining and Metallurgy, Birmingham, England. Apr. 23-25.

96. B.W. Dunning, Jr., F. Ambrose and H.V. Makar (1983). *Distribution and Gold and Silver in Mechanically Processed Mixed Electronic Scrap*. USBM, RI 6788.

97. F. Ambrose and B.W. Dunning, Jr. (1980). Mechanical processing of electronic scrap to recover precious metal bearing concentrates. *Precious Metals*. Proceedings of the 4th International Precious Metals Institute Conference, Toronto, June. Pergamon Press, Oxford, pp. 67-76.

98. System Redoma. *The Proven Solution for Efficient and Profitable Cable Recycling*. Screen and Conveyor Sales Ltd. pamphlets.

99. E. Laursens Maskinfabrik. Eldan Separation Systems pamphlets. Morrison, Marshall and Hill Ltd.

100. Scandinavia Recycling AB, pamphlet.

101. J. Warczok, A. Pers and Z. Smiesczek (1990). Processing of cable scrap in Poland. *Recycling of Metalliferrous Materials*. Institution of Mining and Metallurgy, Birmingham, England. Apr. 23-25.

102. Bradbury, Gotham, Wudyka. *Electrostatic Separation for Plastic from Metal after Granulator*. United States Patent 3

941 684. See ref. 7.

103. F.S. Knoll and J.B. Taylor (1985). Advances in electrostatic separation. *Minerals and Metallurgical Processing.* May, pp. 106-113.

104. Carpco Inc. *Carpco, the Solution to Separation.* Carpco Inc. Bulletin 907.

105. Carpco Inc. *Electrostatic Cleaning of Chopped PE and PVC Wire Tailings.* Carpco Inc. Application Sheet 90703.

106. Carpco Inc. *Electrostatic Cleaning of Chopped PET Bottles.* Carpco Inc. Application Sheet 88702.

107. B. Warner (1991). The tire recycling challenge. *Scrap Processing and Recycling.* Vol. 46, no. 2. Mar/Apr.

108. H. Althaus (1979). *Sportsfield Surface Made from Used Tyres.* See ref. 10.

109. P. Schmidt (1979). *Recycling of Old Rubber - an Example of the Re-use of Old Tyres.* See ref. 10.

110. Newell Engineering Ltd. *Tyre Shredding Plant.* Newell Data Sheet 87/89.

111. Shredtech Ltd. brochure.

112. A. Farahmand and R. Fischer (1979). *Present State of Battery Scrap Processing by Wet Mechanical Methods.* See ref. 10.

113. A.E. La Point. United States Patent 4 018 567. See ref. 7.

114. E.G. Valdez, K.C. Dean and W.J. Wilson (1973). *Use of Cryogens to Reclaim Non-ferrous Scrap Metals.* USBM, RI 7716.

115. D.J. Drage (1975). Assigned to Air Products and Chemicals Inc., United States Patent 3 905 556. Sept. 17. See ref. 7.

116. B.J. Weston (1976). Assigned to Jeno Inc., United States Patent 3 990 641. Nov. 9. See ref. 7.

117. N.R. Braton (1979). *Cryogenic processing.* See ref. 10.

118. F. Ambrose, et al. (1983). Hot-crush technique for separation of cast- and wrought-aluminium alloy scrap. *Conservation and recycling.* Vol. 6, no. 1/2, pp. 63-69.

119. I.G. Belmore (1989). *Reclamation of Copper from Copper*

Plastic Scrap. Research project 89/6. School of Chemical Engineering, University of Birmingham, Feb.

120. J.R. Holmes (1983). *Waste Management: The Options Facing the Public Authorities*. See ref. 21.

121. J.R. Holmes (1981). *Refuse Recycling and Recovery*. John Wiley and Sons Ltd.

122. M.H. Stanczyk and R.S. DeCesare (1985). *Resource Recovery from Municipal Solid Waste*. USBM Bulletin 683.

123. John F. Crawford and Paul G. Smith (1985). *Landfill Technology*. Butterworths.

124. P. Aarne Vasilund (1986). Air classification of shredder refuse. *Conservation and Recycling*. Vol. 9, no. 1, pp. 35-44.

125. R.S. DeCesare, F.J. Palumbo and P.M. Sullivan (1980). *Pilot-scale Studies on the Composition and Characteristics of Urban Refuse*. USBM, RI 8429.

126. P.M. Sullivan, M.H. Stanczyk and M.J. Spendlove (1973). *Resource Recovery from Raw Urban Refuse*. USBM, RI 7760.

127. J.H. Higinbotham (1980). *Recovery of Glass from Urban Refuse by Froth Flotation*. See ref. 13.

128. M.R. Grubbs and Kenneth H. Ivey (1972). *Recovering Plastics from Raw Urban Refuse by Electrodynamic Techniques*. USBM, TPR 63.

129. T.F. Van, ed (1974). *Recycling and disposal of Solid Wastes, Industrial, Agricultural, Domestic*. Ann Arbor Science Publishers, Michigan.

130. J.W. Jenson (1974). Recycling and disposal of waste plastics. See ref. 129.

131. E. Douglas and P.R. Birch (1975). *Recovery of Potentially Usable Materials from Domestic Refuse by Physical Sorting*. See ref. 26.

132. R. New and R. Papworth (1986). *Recovery of Non-Ferrous Metal from Pulverized Refuse - a Feasibility Study*. Warren Spring Laboratory, LR 579(MR)M.

133. J.F. Bernheisel, P.M. Bagalmar and W.S. Parker (1980). *Trommel Processing of Municipal Solid Waste Prior to Shredding.*. See ref. 13.

134. J. Abert (1979). *Separation Processes at Recovery 1.* New Orleans, Louisiana, USA. See ref. 10.

135. H.F. Christensen and R.A. Kenyon (1979). *Monroe County New York Resource Recovery Facility - Program Update and Design/Construction Details.* See ref. 10.

136. L. Spencer (1980). *Monroe County Resource Recovery Facility.* See ref. 13.

137. H.F. Christensen and D.G. Lanni (1979). County to have third generation resource recovery facility. *Public Works.* May.

138. R.A. Dawson (1982). Monroe County, New York, The Hyping of Great Expectations. *Phoenix Quarterly.*

139. N.J. Weinstein and R.F. Toro (1976). *Thermal Processing of Municipal Solid Waste for Resource and Energy Recovery.* Ann. Arbor Science. Michigan.

140. S.H. Russell and M.K. Wees (1980). *Operating Economics of the City of Ames Resource Recovery System.* See ref. 13.

141. Anon (1983). Miami - resource recovery plant claimed as world's most successful. *Scrap Age.* Feb., pp. 126-129.

142. Anon. (1983). Akron RES, once trouble-ridden. Now trouble-free. *Waste Age.* Nov., pp. 22-25.

143. Institution of Mechanical Engineers, Institute of Solid Waste Management (1978). *Refuse Handling and Processing.* IMechE Conference Publications 1978-3. London. May 11.

144. S. Ottewell (1990). Processing packaging plastics. *The Chemical Engineer.* Nov., pp. 19-20.

145. R.J. Wilson, D.M. Squires and T.J. Veasey (1992). A new process for non-ferrous metal recovery from auto shredder reject, using both new and established technology. *Waste Processing and Recycling in MIning and Metallurgical Industries.* Proc. Int. Symp. CIM, Alberta, Canada.

INDEX

For Product Safety Concerns and Information please contact our EU representative GPSR@taylorandfrancis.com Taylor & Francis Verlag GmbH, Kaufingerstraße 24, 80331 München, Germany

Printed and bound by CPI Group (UK) Ltd, Croydon, CR0 4YY

08/05/2025

01864490-0001